Imaging the Journey

...of Contemplation, Meditation, Reflection, and Adventure

by Mark C. Mattes and Ronald R. Darge
Photography by Ronald R. Darge
Prayers by Ronald L. Taylor
Foreword by Kent L. Henning
Concluding Thought by Philip L. Hougen

Lutheran University Press
Minneapolis, Minnesota

Copyright

Imaging the Journey

...of Contemplation, Meditation, Reflection, and Adventure

by Mark C. Mattes and Ronald R. Darge
Photography by Ronald R. Darge
Prayers by Ronald L. Taylor
Foreword by Kent L. Henning
Concluding Thought by Philip L. Hougen

Library of Congress Cataloging-in-Publication data
Mattes, Mark C.
  Imaging the journey-- of contemplation, meditation, reflection, and adventure / Mark C.
  Mattes ; photography Ronald Darge.
    p. cm.
  ISBN-13: 978-1-932688-14-6 (alk. paper)
  ISBN-10: 1-932688-14-5 (alk. paper)
  I. Meditations. I. Darge, Ronald. II. Title.

BV4832.3.M345 2006
242--dc22

                                    2006040878

Lutheran University Press, PO Box 390759, Minneapolis, MN 55439
www.lutheranUpress.org
Manufactured in Hong Kong

Contents

$\mathsf{\mathsf{F}oreword}$ Kent L. Henning

The hectic pace of life leaves precious little time for reflection and introspection. A constant barrage of media messages and information numbs our ability to observe, notice, and concentrate. Sadly, these facts of modern life often prevent us from seeing God's work all around us and "listening" for the lessons and messages embedded therein.

Lutherans, along with several other major denominations, have reverence for God's presence in all of creation. Luther taught us that God reveals himself through many masks, not the least of which is the world around us. Danish Lutherans hold this understanding and pass it on to successor generations through the ever-popular folk tune, "Evening Star." In it, the singer invites nature to "teach me."

Evening star up yonder,
Teach me like you to wander
Willing and obediently
The path that God ordained for me!
Evening star up yonder!

Teach me lonely heather,
Where songbirds nest together,
Though my life should seem unblest,
To keep a song within my breast!
Teach me, lonely heather!

Shady lanes, refreshing,
Teach me to be a blessing
To some weary soul each day,
Friends or foes who pass my way!
Shady lanes, refreshing!

Selected verses from "Evening Star"
Danish Hymn by Christian Richardt

The authors present other verses from this familiar tune in the chapter entitled "Evening Sun." What wonderful reflections on things observed in God's creation!

The authors of this book invite—even challenge—you the reader to *see,* to *observe,* and then to *reflect* on the messages found all around us, in nature as well as in the activities and creations of fellow human beings. The authors' hope is that doing so will enable you the faithful to remain in awe of God's great creative power and therefore remain faithful to God in your journey through life. The authors' purpose fulfills the observation made by Dr. Mattes in the chapter entitled "Temples":

... the distinction between the sacred and the profane, or the spiritual and secular, is artificial. All things in this world reflect the sacredness of God, to some degree or another.

At times, the photography will challenge, even frustrate you. In our fast-paced lives, we want all the answers and we want them right away. As an artist, Pastor Darge has captured images that are abstract or that capture a minute portion of a larger, familiar subject. You will ask, "What is this?" And you may well be frustrated that the photographer does not tell you. At precisely that moment, stop! Pay attention to what *you* think the photograph is or what it represents. What meaning do *you* find in it?

Dr. Mattes's writings provide one—but only one—reflection on the meaning or purpose of each photograph. That reflection may or may not be what Pastor Darge had in mind when he took the photograph. And Dr. Mattes's writing may or may not be what *you* receive as insight from the photograph and reflection. *You,* with your own life experiences and study, bring something to this book.

For example, when I first encountered the photograph and writings in the chapter "Temples," I recalled a recent experience of my own. After visiting a friend in the final hours of his life, and after tearful hugs and handshakes with the man's family, I was drawn to the hospital's chapel like a moth drawn to light. I *needed* to sit, to reflect, to pray, to cry. I needed what Dr. Mattes described: "The church as sanctuary should be a safe place, an icon of God's love. In such an icon, God reaches out to embrace, affirm, and make available his grace."

Yet, in the same chapter, Dr. Mattes reminds us, "As people of faith we share in Christ's continuing ministry in the world as we offer the good news, forgive sins, feed the hungry, visit the prisoner, care for one another, and render justice to the oppressed." His writing prompted my own reflection on Matthew 25 and how that chapter of the Bible shapes my own understanding of vocation. And the juxtaposition of an image of a church sanctuary in a section of the book entitled *"Ministry as Service"* affirms that our relationship with our God includes both work (vocation) and worship.

Another example…in the series of photographs and writings in the section *"Renewal in the Midst of Conflict"* the authors present the cyclical nature of God's creative power. Images of and reflections on a forest fire remind us that new life is created, and sometimes nourished by, a prior death.

As I read this chapter, I could not help but think of other examples of how God's creative power works through cyclical patterns elsewhere in nature. Consider spring with its birth and new growth, followed by summer and its blossoming and maturing processes, followed by fall's harvest of the fruits of summer's labors, followed by death from the cold of winter. And the decay of the previous year's life will nourish new life in the forthcoming spring. This cycle of seasons, of course, results from earth rotating around the sun. The moon's orbit around the earth results in a number of cycles observed on earth. For instance, those who live near an ocean or an estuary can identify the creative power of the cycle of tides.

Pastor Darge's images of a forest fire and Dr. Mattes's reflections suggests that the destruction and rebirth resulting from that inferno can "teach us" (in the tradition of that Danish hymn) about how to live through conflict in our lives.

Yes, *you* must bring your own thoughts and experiences to these images and writings to appreciate this project fully, just as you would to a Bible study at your church. It is my hope that your journey through these images and writings will train your mind to observe God's grace and power beyond the pages of this book. May it help you see again God's presence in his abundant creation. And may those powers of observation and reflection open our lives to the Holy Spirit so that we may—like the Evening Star—"wander willing and obediently the path that God ordained for (us)!"

Introduction

The following meditations and prayers invite the reader into a journey of adventure through reflection on photographic images, meditations and, through these, to scripture. These reflections are guided by Martin Luther's thinking. For Luther, the life of faith is borne in experience. Knowing that God is at life's helm, there is nothing in our experience that we must reject. All human experiences can be seen as details of God's artistry as God is shaping our lives from moment to moment.

Christians have often compared life to a journey or pilgrimage. In light of the gospel, we are already wise to the outcome of the journey. The last judgment has already been rendered for the world. It was spoken when Jesus, dying on the cross, said, "It is finished." In light of the cross, we are all sinners. But, more importantly, we are sinners claimed by God.

It is *only* sinners that God befriends. In light of this truth, we can see life's journey not as a self-fulfilling voyage upward or inward to perfection, but as a pilgrimage outward in honor to God, service to others, and enjoyment of God's good creation.

When not led by this insight, people will attempt to encapsulate experience into an encyclopedic, grand scheme of things, either through their ability to control the world or through their desire to perfect the world. Similar to a gardener who weeds a garden, God prunes us of our self-centered, self-justifying behavior. God is tearing down destructive patterns of behavior so that we can live freely and to the fullest. Luther was confident that if people would be compelled to claim this God-given freedom, then compassion for one's neighbor would spontaneously arise in the heart. He called this experience of dying to self-righteousness and rising to a new life of faith a "theology of the cross." He contrasted this approach to life with the quest for the grand scheme, in either thinking or doing, which he called a "theology of glory."

United by baptism with Jesus in his death and resurrection, we are opened to a new appreciation of the world. We receive a new aesthetic, a new way to appreciate the world for its own sake. This new aesthetic recasts the world, its contents, and its events, so that we are set in a new and clear relationship to it all.

God the Artist also wants to make us artists. Art is inherently communicative. At its root, art means to put or bring something together. Surprisingly, the doing of art is markedly similar to the practice of religion, which aims to connect us to that which binds all things together.

Once completed, a work of art invites probing, discussion, thoughtful awareness, and challenge. It requests that we expand ourselves, move outside our comfort zones. The consummate artist, of course, is God, who continuously creates and upholds the universe.

All human artistry is only done in and through God's artistry. Whether we are aware of it or not, our art imitates God's work in one way or another. Whatever we do that is "original" is initiated, done, and upheld in God. When inspired by both law and gospel, art is done for the sake of honoring God and serving the neighbor.

The contents of this volume have been organized around seven crucial themes selected because they are natural expressions of the authors' callings, which total nearly ten decades of pastoral service, teaching, or administration. The first theme, *a spirituality of communication*, focuses on faith as a receptive openness to the gracious God who speaks to us in all created things. The aim in these reflections is to foster awareness that receptivity is the primary mode of being human. Receptivity to God's promise does not stifle freedom, but secures it. Further, this spiritual awareness challenges the notion that the human is the primary agent who needs to control the world, either through thinking or doing. We are called to be stewards of God's creation, not emperors over it.

The second theme, *the newness of new life*, expands the first by acknowledging that God is both creative and re-creative, initiating all of life and renewing humanity and the earth from the corrosive effects of sin. Human nature does not need to be perfected in order for it to experience salvation. Rather, it needs to be liberated from the prison of self-justifying ways of living, including religious perfectionism. Self-righteousness, we should note, can be found in both religious and non-religious varieties. Set free from sin, the goodness of God's creativity in nature is unleashed. God's love and graciousness does not perfect nature, but liberates it from sin. Nature as coming from God's hand is good in and of itself.

The third theme, *fragmentation and wholeness*, acknowledges that sin results in brokenness. We have not only received violence and brokenness, but have also transmitted them. No one experiences life free from pain. Only God can restore us to integrity and wholeness, permitting us to foster social wellness for others. God does this as God creates new beings, new creations. Even the pain that Jesus received at our hands does not hold back God's love. The empty tomb is the chief gift of God's love.

The next three themes, *ministry as service*, *renewal in the midst of conflict*, and *vocation*, acknowledge that by being embraced by God's love, accepting life on its own terms, we can, in turn, minister in the world. This public, priestly office is presided over by both ordained and lay persons. Daily life and daily ministry will encounter opposition; however, we need not fear conflict because we know that no pain can overpower God's embrace.

The final section, *alpha and omega*, sums up the life of sinners claimed by God's grace. We know our source and our end is in God. Thereby, we can share our unique gifts in the world for the world's well-being.

In Luther's view of creation, all things are capable of serving as God's messengers to us. These photographs, reflections, and prayers seek to convey this communication as well. Their intention is to engage each viewer in a three-way conversation between the artist (the photographer and writers), the work of art (the photographs and meditations), and you the viewers and readers with the intent of helping us discern the work of God in the world and in life. It is through this three-way conversation that artistic endeavor is meaningful and truth is conveyed.

Many of the images are abstract. In a first viewing, you may be inclined to ask, "What is it?" We believe, however, that what needs to be asked is, "What questions does the image provoke or make me want to ask?" Only the viewer can answer that. These images are not designed to limit or encapsulate your experience, but rather to open it up for new horizons of meaning.

Each of the seven main sections is introduced with an image of a concrete, specific artifact or symbol found on the Grand View College campus, celebrating the College's Grundtvigian, Danish heritage. We felt this was appropriate given the fact that many of the meditations have been influenced by this heritage and that all of the authors connected with this volume serve Grand View as teachers, administrators, or advisors.

We hope these images and meditations affirm the old Danish hymn, "Beauty around us, glory above us, Lovely is earth and the smiling skies, Singing we pass along, Pilgrims upon our way, Thro' these fair lands to Paradise!" Thereby, we trust that a meaningful exploration of humanity is possible and that life can be lived zestfully, creatively, and freely.

Be Still

"Be still and know that I am God" (Psalm 46:10). Be silent. Be quiet. Otherwise, you cannot hear.

"Be still." Quit obsessing over the future. We don't own the future. God does. How will you see what God is giving you if you do not open your eyes and listen with your ears?

"Be still." God is speaking to each one of us. No, God is not speaking in the depths of the self, contrary to what many think. Self-talk is never the same as God talking. God is not the self. Rather, God speaks each self into being, together with all other creatures. God is not the insides of our being but the source of our being.

"Be still." God is speaking to you. Where? Everywhere! How? In "all things bright and beautiful, all creatures great and small." God uses the whole of creation to bring us to stillness.

What does God want us to see and to hear? God wants us to see and to hear the delicate beauty of the truth that God is God.

A frozen pond shares in that delicate beauty in shades of color, from dark black to light blue, immersed in icy fissures and the swirl of a twice-frozen eddy. Some would ask, "What can God tell us in frozen slush?" They need to think further. Beneath the slush, the water is calm, quiet, still.

"Be still…be still and know that I am God." If we were never still, how would we ever learn that God is God? After all, life experience will eventually teach us that we cannot be our own gods for ourselves. The Psalmist knew our dependency on God. "He has made us and we are the sheep of his pasture, the flock that God shepherds" (Psalm 100:3). This dependency does not hold us captive, but sets us free.

God wants us to know that he satisfies because he can fill us with delight. God wants us to know that each created thing can sparkle as a reflection of that delight.

What is God doing in the world? God is restoring, renewing, and reclaiming the creation. He is restoring his whole creation and us, his people of faith. Faith gives birth to love. Love gives delight to life!

"Be still and know that I am God." Creation needs restoring. In our sin, we think we can do better at playing God than God can do in being God. Yes, be still and know God! Be still, let God be God for you, and delight will be opened further for each person as well.

Through faith, all our senses—seeing, hearing, touching, tasting, and smelling—will be further opened for pleasure. Is God generous? Yes, God is abundantly generous. "Be still and know that I am God."

Gentle God, awaken our senses and open our hearts to your presence. Free us from the brokenness and distractions that prevent us from hearing your voice and doing your will. Make us still so that we might rejoice in knowing that you are God and delight in what is yet to come. Amen.

A New Spirituality

The attempt at introspection is often counter-productive. The journey within fails to give us an objective perspective by which to evaluate ourselves. It might even suggest that all is hopeless and unsolvable. Seeking relief, we turn to various options for self-help, like New Age spiritualities. These feed the notion that the self is sacred, which in fact aggravates the very self-centeredness that is a source of our unrest. Such "spirituality" is an internal work, and, through it, one is offered a buffet line of self-enhancing options.

The upshot is that in the modern world, self-development is no longer an option but a requirement. Thereby, it becomes a burden. We are like Atlas, loading the responsibility of our worth on ourselves alone. The weight of the world rests all on our shoulders. Where spirituality is seen as a menu of religious options, it exacerbates a problem. It masks self-centeredness as spirituality. The self needs liberation from even itself, if it is to be free.

Spiritual unrest needs a better diagnosis than what these therapies provide. In faith, we can affirm that we are part and parcel of all created life. Independently of God and the world, the self can know nothing true about itself. The Psalmist tells us to number our days (Psalm 90:12). God alone provides the standard for measurement, the only basis by which to evaluate and know ourselves. Only God can free us from self-centeredness and open us to creation. Freed from the burden of the self, we can look outside ourselves and discover new meaning. Freed from self-concern, we can perceive the many rich subtleties that enlarge our experience of life.

Through the interplay of depth, texture, color, and natural lighting within the photograph, insights emerge to bring us to the edge of diversity and possibilities. To where is your attention drawn? Does the shaft of light touch the floor…of sand? To the textures of weathering from water and wind long gone? Do you drift past the canvasses of light and darkness, shade and transparency? What questions does it make you want to ask?

Life seldom offers options that are clearly defined. Often our decisions must be made in circumstances in which we lack a clear direction. We are invited to walk by faith, not by sight (2 Corinthians 5:7). Such an invitation is designed to help us find gentleness in life. This is something that anxiety, with its distorted favoring of all or nothing thinking, knows little about.

To be human is to be concerned. We have control over some matters and no control over others, particularly the most important. As Reinhold Niebuhr prayed, we need to have the serenity to accept what we cannot change, the courage to change what we can, and the wisdom to know the difference.

Holy One, touch our lives with new light and make of us a new creation. Free us from the self-centeredness that sometimes makes it difficult to see new possibilities. Help us to see anew "who we are" while never forgetting "to whom we belong." So be it.

Wisdom in Meditation

The Psalmist says, "Thy word is a lamp unto my feet and a light to my path" (Psalm 119:105). God's word imparts God's Spirit, who illuminates our lives and the world. The task of integrating one's life and world through reflection is challenging, but it can also serve to spread light. It helps us grow in wisdom.

Counter to how we usually think it is done, meditation is not a purely internal task. Rather, meditation is always accountable to external sources, most importantly to scripture, but also to wider Christian traditions across time and in many cultures, as well as to creation. Scripture, however, has the primary say in these matters. It grants us a path in life, which, apart from scripture, can seem like a maze.

Scripture helps us to recognize the world as God's creation since it teaches us to affirm God's providence in all things (Psalm 19). Meditation on the scriptures is indeed personal, but also profoundly social, helping us to interpret God, others, and the world.

Prior to Christ's second coming, St. Paul tells us, we "see through a glass dimly." It is only when Christ returns that we shall see God "face to face." Furthermore, Paul continues, "Now, we know only in part; then we shall know even as we are fully known" (1 Corinthians 13:12).

Glass is not always transparent. It may be etched, colored, or opaque, thus obscuring an aspect of a work of art. In like manner, Paul insists that although the world finds Christ foolish, due to the shame of the cross, *Christ is our wisdom* (1 Corinthians 1:18-25).

God is always at work, ever nurturing us to be more Christlike in faith and love. God uses many means to renew us. Indeed, all creation serves at God's behest in this matter, impacting, instructing, and transforming our lives into ones of faith and service.

"We walk by faith, not by sight" (2 Corinthians 5:7). Paul does not mean that we don't see. Instead, he means that our confidence in God permits us to see the world and ourselves as they truly are. We can see past the distortions and false idols by which we aim to shore up faltering self-concepts or legitimate power over others. In such transparency, as illuminated by God, our distortions are exposed and painful. Through God's light, we experience a death to a sinful self.

In this image, light at the center, with its various refractions, indicates the back and forth nature of human meditation. Surprisingly, reflection is not just immediate. Instead it is always reflection upon previous reflections, whether one's own or that of others.

In this image, we see the prospect of purple repeated in new vistas despite (or because of) the darkness. From the light at the core of the image, we can discern the symbol of a lamp, the ancient symbol for wisdom, suggesting truth that God imparts, most clearly in scripture, but also in all things.

Finally, at the bottom of the image, royal purple radiates the color of sacramental wine, the means of God's gift of forgiveness and new life orally imparted to us. The gift of God's grace makes the fragmentations of our lives and world less threatening, and even inviting.

Guide, O God of Wisdom, our feeble efforts to make sense of this world. Let those efforts begin and end with our acknowledgment of you as the source of all wisdom. Help us to grow in faith and love so that we might become more courageous people of service to others. Amen.

Communication

O taste and see how gracious
the Lord is, blessed are those
who trust in God. (Psalm 34:8)

In scripture, mountains serve as places where God communicates. On Sinai, God gives the law. At another mountain, Jesus gave his famous sermon. In this image, the reflection from Half Dome in Yosemite also shares truth. It is a way for God to speak to us.

To be human is to communicate, even if we do not always understand or appreciate what the communication is about. As communicators, we echo the efforts of all other created things in the desire to reach out to others. Most importantly, God is reaching out to us. All created things serve as masks of God. God is hidden everywhere in creation. All things speak both God's judgment upon us and his providential grace to us.

Like Moses, we discover that God communicates to us even with his "backside" (Exodus 33:17-34:9). And, like Jacob, we often encounter God in a power struggle (Genesis 32:22-30). Jacob's very nickname, "Israel," means one who wrestles with God. This struggle, however, is not always clear. We can be confused about the one with whom we wrestle: is it God or a demon? This ambiguity is overcome only in the cross of Jesus as the epitome of God's self-giving love.

God communicates bodily. God's message always comes through physical means. Whether with baptismal water, the bread and wine of the Lord's Supper, or the voice of a preacher, God's word is spoken bodily. There is no pure, disembodied spirituality. God loves matter.

God's love finds its way to us through human means, including culture and history. It is well said that the universe is not made of atoms, but of stories. Even atoms are to be understood by their histories, if they are to be understood at all.

Worship, like Eden, ought to be a place of sensual delight, a garden of smells, sounds, sight, drama, and tastes among other things. In these earthy realities, God is generous. Symbolism should not be disdained in worship.

In worship, we are restored to creation. In worship, God is serving us.

Worship must never convey the economic system of the shopping mall. The mall promises only a materialistic utopia. Its sensuality is an empty, false imitation of the abundant blessings of God. The mall glorifies human control over creation. It worships our excesses. In contrast, worship shaped by Jesus' cross acknowledges all things as the gracious gift of a merciful God.

In sum, worship symbols and signs point to the truth of: "come to the waters, you who have no money, come and receive what is free" (Isaiah 55:1).

Great Communicator, we rejoice in the gift of communication which you have given to humankind. Let that gift speak to us of your grace through words and deeds, through the sacraments and the arts. Challenge us to explore new means and methods to communicate the story of your salvation. Strengthen our appreciation for the diversity of your creation and the varied forms of expression that are manifest by that diversity. Help us to listen more patiently, hear more clearly, and communicate more compassionately. Amen.

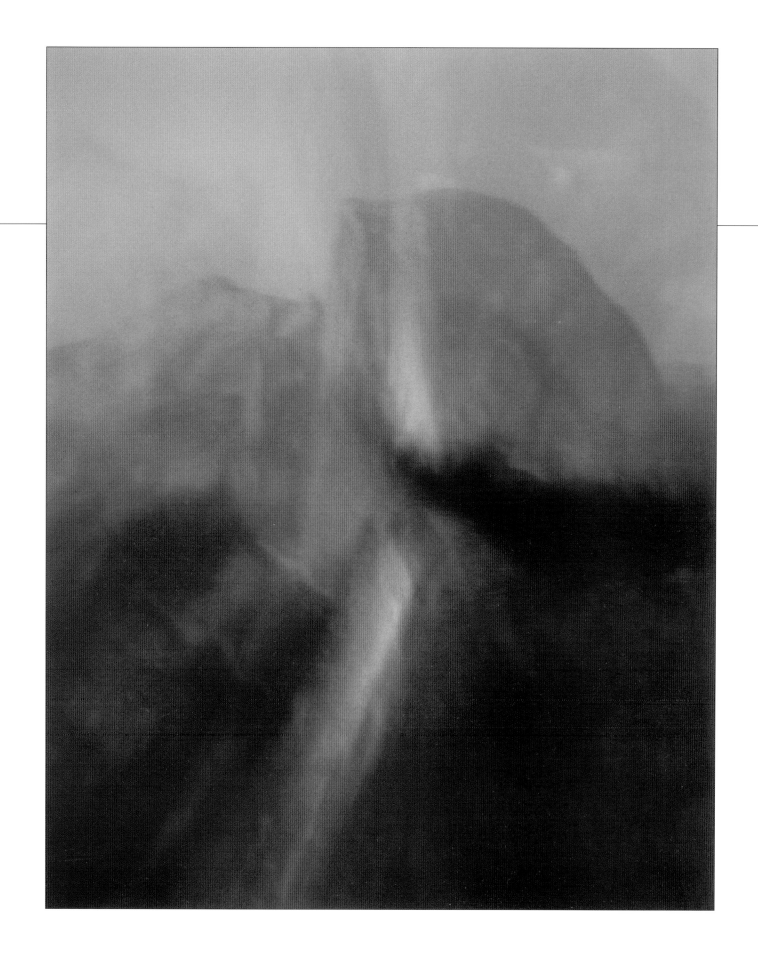

Receive

The Lord gives his beloved sleep.
(Psalm 127:2)

The Lord almighty grant us a quiet
night and peace at the last.

Guide us waking, O Lord, and guard
us sleeping, that awake we may watch
with Christ and asleep we may rest in
peace.*

The smoke rising in this image is not random. It is a message sent from one group of people to another group who understand its message. This particular message is being sent at dusk, the time to settle down for rest.

Very often, we take sleep for granted. Yet, what is more important for work than a good night's rest? Refreshed, we are ready to take on our daily tasks.

In literature, darkness is often associated with uneasiness and danger. In sleep, we have no control. It behooves us to entrust ourselves to God's care, confident that we will be safe through the night.

We tend to think of sleep as passive. In some ways it is. In sleep "self," with all its ambitions, doubts, goals, and insecurities, evaporates. Ironically, in sleep, with such an evaporated self, we are rejuvenated. In sleep we are not resistant to God.

So sleep is not unproductive. When our agency is quieted, God goes to work. We sometimes wake with answers to problems that before seemed unsolvable. Sleep permits insights to come to us from beyond our conscious efforts to solve problems.

God grants rest. Because we are so focused on our work, we moderns are most apt to forget the third commandment: "Remember the Sabbath day to keep it holy." Only with rest can we fully honor God. The Sabbath is a gift from a faithful God who provides what we need. We can live because we don't have to work ourselves to death.

Dusk is when stars appear. Stars affirm a gracious order and providence. They confirm the truth that "the light shines in the darkness" (John 1:5). Like the smoke, dusk invites communication. It invites a message sent, received, and understood by those who offer thanks, praise, petitions, lamentation, and confession. Dusk can be a time of hope. It can specifically point us to God's unfailing care. In God's promise, even darkness can be illuminating.

Lutheran Book of Worship (Minneapolis: Augsburg Publishing House and Board of Publication, Lutheran Church in America, p.154; p. 160)

Almighty God, quiet our bodies and spirits that you might enter our hearts more fully. In that peace, order our lives to receive your message of love and hope. Refresh and prepare us for the days that are yet to come and grant to us the peace and tranquility that only comes from rest in you. Amen.

Delight

"You may freely eat of every tree of the garden" God told Adam and Eve, "but of the tree of the knowledge of good and evil you shall not eat, for in the day you eat of it you shall die" (Genesis 2:16-17).

Such is the declaration of God. If we as creatures seek a role for ourselves in the garden that belongs to the Creator alone, all creation will resist us. This will result only in our demise. Nevertheless, note this well. God begins his command with a promise first. You may *freely* eat…. God is generous. God provides enough of the earth's fruits to meet our needs. God desires that we enjoy this bounty. God grants permission for such enjoyment. We are given space and time for delight.

Martin Luther noted that if a single grain could speak, it would say, "Eat me, enjoy me, and through me serve your neighbor." We need not pit delight against service, aesthetics against ethics. God's promise, received in faith, reaches a person from the outside in. God's word coming from outside us in scripture, in the sacraments, or through a preacher's voice renews us and refocuses us towards others' needs.

To savor the delights of this earthly garden, and to give God glory for it, is far removed from the abuse of this good earth. No enjoyment of this world, this treasure, this gift, is compatible with our perceived "need" to pollute the planet resulting from our perceived "need" to control the earth.

Jesus offers these healing words, "*Ephatha*, be opened" (Matthew 7:34) in order to release all our human senses to delight. God is no miser. God is love. Love wants the beloved to delight in what is given. This delight is offered with reciprocated love, respect, and honor to the Holy and Mighty Giver of all things. Thanksgiving, praise, service, and obedience are the most appropriate responses by those made in God's image.

Merciful Father, we give thanks for the goodness and wonder of your creations. May our delight and use of these gifts bring joy to you and to one another. Bless and prosper our efforts to be wise stewards of these creations. Let the beauty and majesty of your creation be a constant reminder of your generosity and your love for us. In Jesus we pray.

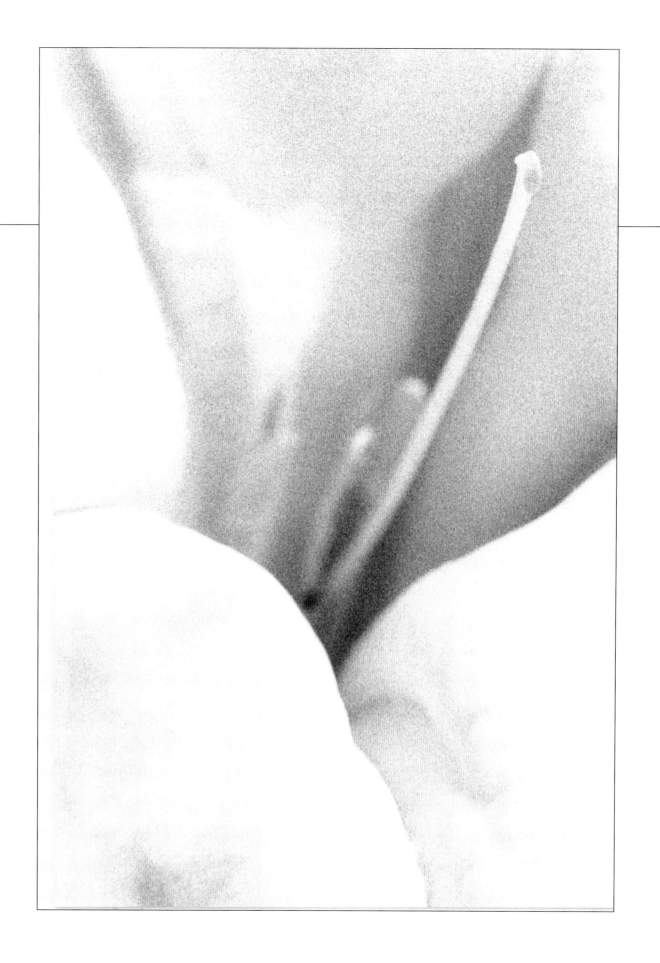

Pentecost

Isaiah proclaims, "The earth shall be full of the knowledge of the Lord as the waters cover the sea" (Isaiah 11:9).

Ours is a Pentecost world. Too quickly that can be forgotten! Jesus Christ does not continue to hang on the cross. His atoning work has been accomplished. "It is finished," he said. To overcome sin, death, and the devil—Christ's work—Jesus tasted death. Thus the victory of Christ lives in Easter glory. The Pentecost Spirit shines through the empty tomb to illuminate and nourish the world.

Danish theologian N. F. S. Grundtvig said we live in a day "full of grace." A day "full of grace" is God's good news being shared daily throughout the world. It is a word that transforms us before and by means of the cross. Baptismally we die to self-centeredness and rise to a new life. In this new life we are selflessly engaged.

The color of the season of Pentecost is green. We are drawn to a world that God is greening. God is awakening new purpose, new joy, and new hope throughout the world. God is inviting us to community and celebration. God seeks to renew the earth so that it might fulfill its destiny to reflect God's very image.

Often our contemporary world emphasizes the economic quest of self-fulfillment, resulting in domination over the earth, and bypassing the needs of others. In a world which God greens, we deforest and defrost. In a world of delicate balance between the atmosphere and the surface of the planet, we warm globally.

As stewards of God and one another, what are we called to do? We are called to stay true to the story and vision of Pentecost. In light of God's grace and power we can acknowledge the world's folly when it attempts to establish a security and reputation that only works us harm.

During those eras in which it seems that God has abandoned his purpose for the world, when people fall into discouragement, we must hear again the promise that God intends to bring his creation to fruition. God is stirring his church to her mission. God is calling us to the story and vision of Pentecost. We can embrace the mission of sharing Christ and his goodness, and offer hope for the world, and the invitation to live as stewards of God's good earth.

Holy Spirit, call us anew to the story and vision of Pentecost. Let Jesus' death on the cross continue to transform our lives and awaken us to new opportunities to praise and serve you. Renew and strengthen your Church on earth that she might continue to be a beacon of light and hope for all those who suffer and seek your mercy. Come Holy Spirit, come.

The Newness of the New Life

The Cross

In the varied shadows of this image, we first take notice of a figure, head slightly lowered, arms and hands dropping to the side, and dressed in his Sunday best. The figure is seated and supported on something we do not see. Nothing is quite as opaque as a sculptured representation of the human form, especially from the back.

At the lower right, facing the man, one can discern a cross of light. The cross shines on all people whether they are aware of it or not. The cross discloses human impotence and guilt. No one can accuse another person of crucifying Jesus. His death is one's own crime. Remember the words of the Good Friday hymn, "'Twas I, Lord Jesus, I it was denied thee, I crucified Thee!" (*Lutheran Book of Worship*, #123).

His death, however, brings about our death too. His death ends our empty self-justifying, self-serving life and exposes it as a caricature of real life. Our Sunday best is nothing less than a pretense in the light of the cross.

Focused on the man's back, the image implies shame and guilt. While noticeable only as a shape or form, the view captures our attention. It is unashamedly seeking the promise of new life, *a gift only given to sinners.*

Sin is not vice as opposed to virtue. Rather, sin is unbelief in opposition to faith. Surprisingly, it is not we who make ourselves to be sinners. Rather, God is in charge of even that for he gives the law that reveals our sin. Yet, God is making us to be sinners of a certain sort, ones who trust him in all things, especially for righteousness.

The nothingness of sin is comparable to that nothingness out of which God makes worlds. Just as God creates all that is from nothing at all, God is making faithful people from the nothingness of sin. When we no longer look to our own resources, we can begin to accept God's deity and holiness in our lives. We can then entrust our lives to his management. God opens our senses, our intentions, and our understanding through his promise, "I am your God. I will provide for you in all things." This promise allows us to join God in service in the world.

God sustains us both in our guilt and in our hope. The cross not only accuses us, but also imparts new life to us. It is God's commitment to us that not even our rejection of God's generosity can separate us from him (Romans 8:35). How shall we respond to such generosity?

Often, we talk about "light" that suddenly dawns upon us as we realize something in a new way. "Light" that is transparent. "Light" that is obscured. "Light" that is enlightening. What can we do with such generosity? Revel in it.

Heavenly Father, let the cross be a constant reminder of the sacrifice you made for us and the promise of new life which your sacrifice made possible. Cleanse our lives from the thoughts, words, and deeds which obscure your message of hope and wholeness. Steady and strengthen our trust in you. Amen.

Resurrection

Jesus promises, "I am the resurrection and the life" (John 11:25).

The Easter acclamation, "The Lord is risen; He is risen indeed," is the truth that sustains us in the midst of our culture's darkness and the darkness of our own fear, remorse, and anger.

The abstract image before us bears the patibulem of what is seen as a crucifix. The lower portion of the image appears as two legs in motion, as though Christ is emerging from the tomb. He is the resurrected one, the one who has taken the punishment of human sin, borne it bodily, endured its abuse, and has brought evil to its end. Now, Christ is raised by the Spirit, who has urged him forward as God's light, conquering the evil of darkness and violence everywhere.

No darkness can envelope the light of Christ. We miscalculate matters if we accentuate the power of evil. Evil has been conquered through Jesus' resurrection. The head of the serpent has been crushed (Genesis 3:16-17). In baptism, united to Christ, we share in the vanquishing of evil. This is confessed when we renounce all the forces of evil, the devil, and all his empty promises. Baptism yokes us to Christ's resurrection life (Romans 6:4).

Jesus' whole ministry involved exorcism, the casting out of evil, the casting out of demons. Modern people should not construe such exorcism as frivolous. The modern world has produced more than its share of demonic power. Christ the conqueror of evil is gaining turf in the world then and now in order to establish peace for all.

To renounce evil is to trust in Christ Jesus and to look to his promise: "Lo, I am with you always, even until the close of the age" (Matthew 28:20). As German theologian Oswald Bayer notes, between the manger and the cross, God is eternally for you. St. Paul affirms, "If God is for us, who can be against us? He who did not spare his Son, but gave him up for us all, will he not also give us all things with him?" (Romans 8:31).

Christ has emerged. Christ is unbound. God is making good on his promise.

Now, what will happen to the world?

Risen Lord, may the light of the cross overcome the darkness that threatens to overpower us. Help us to recognize and reject the evil which exists in our own lives and in the lives of our neighbors. Draw us into the light of the resurrection and your promise of new life. "He is risen; He is risen indeed, Alleluia. Alleluia. Alleluia."

A Free Life

We are justified, saved, forgiven by God's grace alone through faith alone in Jesus Christ. God claims only sinners as his own.

We have a difficult time accepting that. Would God really toss out his grace on unappreciative sinners? Everyone knows that there is no free lunch. Everyone knows that.

Isn't there something I can do? Surely God expects something of me?

It's hard to accept it: unless God saves us, we won't have a chance at salvation. We do not want to let go of our control over life. Even this urge shows us the depth of our predicament and reinforces that only faith will suffice in our relationship with God.

Now, saved by faith, the question, "what do we *want* to do in light of God's love," is appropriate.

St. Paul "presses on" to make fulfillment in Christ his own. "Beloved, I do not consider that I have made it my own; but this one thing I do: forgetting what lies behind and straining forward to what lies ahead, I press on toward the goal for the prize of the heavenly call of God in Christ Jesus" (Philippians 3:12-14).

Life in Christ is the horizon in which we do things. Life in Christ allows us to live freely. We have the assurance that the last judgment has been rendered *now*. To the guilty, God grants forgiveness. To the marginalized, God grants hope. To the broken in spirit, God grants the promise of a new spirit. Even to the dead, God grants new life.

God not only forgives us but also forgives the entire world. Are we in a position to condemn when God has already embraced others? It is too late for such condemnation.

So, how shall we live in light of God's unconditional commitment? We have gifts and we can offer them freely to others. We can live open to this world in all its fullness and diversity. We can enjoy it as a work of art in the making.

In life God teaches us that, even though we compete, we need not be competitors. How? Because, we have nothing ultimate at stake in what we offer. Ultimate matters have already been settled.

In racing, we compete, not because we need to be first, but for the challenge, the fun, and the gifts we offer. Sharing gifts, we are set from self-centeredness. God opens us to a completely free, spontaneous life, oblivious to rewards.

A bicycler does not think about balancing the bicycle. While racing, hearts pound, bodies sweat, and riders are alert. Balance itself takes over. One is never more alive than when participating in such a sport, with only the goal on one's mind.

The Spirit animates us, giving us life, sustaining us as we offer our gifts. What more could we want than to share our gifts in the world, to the very end?

Inspire us, dear Savior, with the freedom that is ours through faith in you. Help us to exercise that freedom with the wisdom and compassion that will bring glory to you and healing to humankind. Give us the strength to press on with the race that lies ahead knowing that faith in you has already secured for us the prize of eternal life. Amen.

Forgiven—Free

"The wages of sin is death" (Romans 6:23). We are apt to think that St. Paul is exaggerating. In our "enlightened" twenty-first century, we are quick to name death as natural. However, if it is so "natural," then why does it evoke guilt? With death, we can never make good on our responsibilities, nor can others make good on their responsibilities to us. Death closes out our commitments.

Four decades ago, Karl Mennenger asked, "Whatever became of sin?" The question is even more relevant today. It seems that Americans are not sinners. Instead, we are victims of abuse, not perpetrators.

When that mindset takes root, the gospel is perverted from being an "emancipation proclamation" that sets us free from sin, death, and the accusing law into a self-help program for coping in a stressful world. Or, it is touted as the blueprint for constructing an ideal world where peace and justice or true morality will incontestably reign.

Is it possible that our "officially optimistic" society is wrong in trivializing sin? Whistling in the dark will not make the darkness disappear.

We can get a clue about the power of sin when we look at death. There is certainly enough death to go around. Even young people are taking their own lives as well as others'.

Can we really separate sin from death? True, sin is its own punishment. But that only reinforces the relation between sin and death. Sin is death and not only the crime that is punished with death. Far from being natural, death is "guilt made visible," as Catholic theologian Karl Rahner put it.

Martin Luther distinguished between the "death God works," which is God's just punishment on sinners who all deserve death, from the "death God finds," which is the cycle of violence and retaliation that we constantly perpetrate on each other, and through which God punishes us. Insofar as we sin—as we inescapably will—we cannot avoid either one of these deaths.

"The wages of sin is death, but the free gift of God is eternal life through Jesus our Lord." Into the death that God is working and the death that God finds, Jesus Christ is born, is one with us, and is made a sinner for us. Through this, God effectuates the grand reversal. Jesus' death is the *death of death*. He is the Lamb of God who takes away the sin of the world (John 1:29).

There is no theory to explain this at-one-ment (atonement). Instead, God simply chooses sinners to be one with him. Our sin, in all its ugliness, is not the last word or power. Nor is death. No, the last word is from Jesus' lips, "It is finished." And, within that sentence is a new beginning, the promise of a new heaven and a new earth that shall come.

In Jesus Christ, God looks at us through his Son. In God's strange, but joyous, economic system, our death is exchanged for Christ's life, our unrighteousness for his righteousness, our despair for his joy. We are liberated in the words: "I therefore declare unto you the entire forgiveness of all your sins."

The Son makes you free! And "if the Son makes you free, you will be free indeed" (John 8:36).

Lord, free us from the disfiguring power of sin that is ever present in our lives. Heal our brokenness, lift our spirits, and set our sights on you. Let the liberating power of your forgiving grace fill us with new life. Amen.

IN HIM
ALL THINGS
COHERE

Healing

38

In sorrow, we speak through our tears. Tears are the natural result of a rift in our hearts. Our hearts interconnect us with those whom we mourn in ways that we do not fully understand. In loss, we sense aloneness, alienation. Words seem unable to express or relieve us of grief. In our deepest loss it seems that we are solely dependent on our own resources.

This is where we are wrong. Recall the story of Elijah's departure into heaven in a whirlwind. He left behind him a faithful friend and true disciple, Elisha. Elisha knew that he would need everything he could get from Elijah to carry on the ministry. Before Elijah's departure, Elisha's request to Elijah was to "inherit a double share of your Spirit" (2 Kings 2:9). Elijah's promise to Elisha, his spiritual son, was that he would not leave him (2 Kings 2:2, 4, 6). He also promised Elisha power "if you see me as I am being taken from you" (2 Kings 2:9).

The Bible does not record Elisha's inner sorrow, but he must have been in grief. He knew he would miss his spiritual father. Yet, because of effective mentoring, Elisha is more secure than he realizes. Elijah had built into him an integrity strong enough to withstand the heat of social controversy.

Elisha did in fact see Elijah's ascent to heaven and received the promised spiritual power. Nonetheless, in grief, Elisha cried out, "Father, father! The chariots of Israel and its horsemen!" His grief was visible: "when he could no longer see him, he grasped his own clothes and tore them in two pieces" (2 Kings 2:12).

The loss we feel the most deeply concerns those to whom we look for the most support. Lamentation only imperfectly expresses our deepest grief. Yet, we are able to face the darkness because of the support that mentors have given us. God's power, symbolized in Elijah's mantel, which Elisha inherits, gives us the ability to face emptiness and assures us that no woundedness finally defines our life.

Darkness is permitted only because it is defined by light. There is always more light in life than what we are able to realize or understand. Loss, healing, repair? We shall only find healing in the light of the mantel and the promise of God that will never fade.

God of Mercy, touch us with the healing power of your Spirit. Give us friends and mentors to lighten the burdens we bear. Lift up those who are bowed down. Comfort those who mourn. Heal those in pain and anguish. Grant relief and refreshment to those in trouble. Wrap your cloak of love around us and grant us peace. Amen.

No Answer, only the Answerer

Among the colorful bubbling mud pots, heated crystalline pools, and paradoxical contrasting beauty, how does anyone ever forget the choking sulfurous smell of Yellowstone? Minerals, combined with the heat of subterranean energy and the power of gravity, makes for a setting of nature's creative sculptural beauty carved by the erosion of wind and heated mineral water.

However, sulfur pools do not energize life. Sulfur pools take from life. The dead trees testify to the silent poison. Yet, by contrast, healthy trees stand close like sentinels over the deceased vegetation.

What is God of the good earth doing? Are the pools of death a parable of our wrestling with the God of life and death? Why is God's creative activity so ambiguous? Why is God's gift of life always simultaneously marked with death? Must the dead only provide food for the living? Does death need life and life need death?

Isaiah wrote, "*Truly, you are a God who hides himself,* O God of Israel, the Savior…." (Isaiah 45:15). God is hidden because he will have us to be a people who live from faith alone, not sigh.. God wills life, not death, but God can only destroy what is not life-giving, if life is to be preserved.

There seems to be a correlation with relationships here. We also need others (life), yet others bring grief and pain (death). The gift of intellect is glorious (life), and yet may be the perpetrator of great anxiety or evil purposes (death). Goodness is mixed with delight on the one hand, and disease and decay on the other.

Who would not wish to have, as the physicist Stephen Hawking seeks, a grand unified theory of everything? Who would not wish to know the mind of God? If we knew God's mind, perhaps we could defend the goodness of life against every challenge to this conviction. We could thereby defend God. But, there just seems to be no such defense in the face of either natural disasters, such as a tsunami or hurricane, or the depths of human atrocities, such as "killing fields" and holocaust gas chambers.

All seek to affirm life's goodness, whether they believe in God or not. We want to affirm this goodness in the face of threatening violence and chaos, yet, no matter how much we want a comprehensive answer to the pain that we see or feel, we are given no such answer. Like Job, we receive no answer for why the good suffer while the evil prosper.

Ever dealing with ambiguity, we only receive the *One who Answers*. There is no void with respect to our questions. God himself is the *Answerer* and God speaks to us. We do not get the explanation that we might want. But, instead, we get a relationship. We receive the hope that God will support us no matter what happens

The goodness of life can only be affirmed by faith. Faith is enough.

The only God we will ever know is a God who hides himself. We trust the promise, hidden in creation, vouchsafed on the cross that God will forgive, heal, and provide for us a worthwhile life.

Christ Jesus, amid the starkness of death and the ambiguities of life, help us to listen for the call of your voice. Let us reject the thoughts and behaviors which make it difficult to answer your call and oftentimes poison our relationship with you and with one another. Strengthen our faith, enhance our willingness to listen, and empower us to do the good you call us to do. Amen.

Worth

Death is the biggest challenge to the heroic belief that "I count." Death raises a question to this primal faith: do you really count? Or are you not merely food for worms?

Gravestones serve as memorials to people's lives. They symbolize the abiding worth of the dead. A tomb serves not only to help the living remain in touch with the dead, but it also testifies to the integrity and value of a life.

Ten thousand years ago glaciers covered the land where many of our cemeteries are located in North America. What will become of this same land in another ten thousand years?

Wealth and social standing are not of abiding value. Rather, one's true worth is found in that God claims a sinner as his own. No other final value to life can be found. One is a sinner even in the poverty of one's own resting place. Dust you are, and to dust you shall return. Still, from the dust of our last remains, God redeems to new life.

God knows every hair of our heads! God will provide for us even as God provides for the sparrow (Matthew 10:31). Unlike the sparrows, though, we are the ones of little faith who fret about our status, and even our legacy.

The memorial in our image is not made of marble. Rather, it is made of wood and shaped in cruciform style. The memorial's consistency makes no difference. Our lives are secure from meaninglessness in Jesus' promise, "I am the resurrection and the life" (John 11:25).

So then, what is important for one's life? It is following through on the question, how can I serve and give back to this world? Since my worth is secure in Christ, I don't need to secure status before others. I am free to serve.

Free us, Holy One, from the temptation to seek recognition by the possessions we accumulate, the accomplishments we achieve, or the people we know. Help us to rejoice in the good news that our worth has already been secured by your death and resurrection. Let the liberating presence of the cross raise us up to a new life of service to you and to our neighbors. Let it be so.

The Whole Person

Human life is fragmented. We especially try to understand ourselves in those times and events that fracture us. We attempt to find our voice despite the hurt and despair which too often mark our lives. During such turmoil, we cannot help but wonder what life in God will be like after the close of our earthly days. Will we experience the wholeness we seek?

Ironically, the only hope for wholeness in this life comes in parts. After we undergo significant life experiences, we can look back and discern threads of purpose. Fortunately, God has committed himself to us, even when it seems that all is against us (Romans 8:31). During times of trial, it is to God's promise that we must cling. Even when this promise seems elusive, we can look to the gospel and be confident that we are in the care of a loving and gracious God.

The image of petrified wood, in color, texture, and fissures, illustrates the process of the journey of life. It can provide us with insights and clues into God at work in and through our lives. Just as the fissures belong to the overall experience of the rock, all our irrational drives, fears, and remorse do not frustrate the power of God's steadfast, unconditional love to bring wholeness to our lives.

The rock's color, rich with minerals, is earthy brown, red, and yellow. The roughness has been smoothed over, leaving a pleasing texture, yet gnarled features remain. The deep fissures and rough edges are made more visible. Similarly, in our lives, God is able to redeem pain and wounds.

Rock seems inert, not alive. At the molecular level, though, rock is pulsating with energy, just like our own bodies. The living and the non-living are thought to be opposites, but in truth they are not. At the molecular level they both share the same energy. Furthermore, they are interdependent on each other. For that very reason, we can interpret rocks in light of human traits and human traits in light of rocks. Remember, the Psalmist compares God to a rock (Psalm 18:2)!

Not primarily what we do but what we suffer allows God to sculpt beauty in and through us. Not only our virtues but even our vices become profound ways by which God brings change in the world. Because God is making all things to "work together for good" (Romans 8:28), even our sin or our suffering cannot thwart his purposes.

The gnarledness of the petrified wood becomes inseparable from the character of the wood as a whole. Likewise, our weakness, faults, and misdeeds need not be shunned, but can be affirmed as directing us to those overall positive traits that God is crafting in us.

This is not said so that we might become lazy and revel in our less desirable traits. Rather, it is to recognize that none of our traits can foil God's power at work within us.

God's goal for us is to be whole and at peace. God's work is outside of our control. When we catch glimpses of this beauty, which will only be perfected in the after-life, we cannot help but respond to God with gratitude and service.

Loving God, craft in us a new life—a life of peace and wholeness. Free us from those thoughts and actions which serve to fragment our lives and our relationship with you. Smooth out the rough edges of our lives and create in us a new spirit. Guide us with the assurance that you are at work in our lives. Amen.

Courage to Be

t is natural to want to turn aside from this image. We are repulsed by the disfiguring presented here. The message of this image is offensive and threatening. Here we see a woman who has been defiled and permanently marked, from the abdomen and stomach, to the core of her person.

The violence she has suffered, however, does not define her being. The image conveys hope and power as well. Her legs are planted defiantly, illuminated and supported by light, as if expressing the affirmation of new life, as indicated by the twist of the knot above the wound. It all displays a remarkable view of resilience.

To be defiled and defined by violence is a life experience that all too many people share. Despair leads one to be labeled by victimization. Although violence is never explained, it is possible to continue to affirm life by the power found in God's promise always to be with us, rather than to wallow in self-pity or contempt.

Many wish to hide their wounds, which is understandable. To wear one's wounds publicly could trigger further retaliation, hurt, or pity from others. We wish to shelter ourselves from pain, thereby adding deception to deception and one living only a pretence of life.

Some wounds cannot be hidden. They are simply too definitive of one's life, too real. To succumb to the shame of such a wound is to be consigned to relive and replay the role of victim. The answer is not to mask such pain, but to rise up and walk. It is to live in the promise of God, even if one never receives a reason for the pain. The Crucified understands our plight.

In such woundedness, one can discern who one is by discerning *whose* one is. Disfigured, but not destroyed, we can receive God's promise which renews and restores identity. God's promise is always stronger than our wounds. Such wounds do not rob us of the new life, as indicated by the knot in the image. Indeed, such wounds are unable to deter us from new ventures in life that are affirmed in the twist within the wood and its up-reaching spirit.

Where there is a wound there is a void. How definitive will the void be in one's life? Will it continue as unremitting anger or unresolved anxiety? Will the void ever fade? There is a promise stronger than any emptiness: God's promise. In God's faithfulness is the light of hope, the strength of one's spirit, and the love to carry us forward.

ree us, dear Father, from the disfiguring presence of sin in our lives. Heal our wounded bodies and lift our spirits. Give us the courage to become all that you created us to be. Help us live our lives in the presence of your promise and the life-giving hope offered in that promise which is Christ. Amen.

Venture Forth

The rock, bathed in light, is simultaneously at rest and in motion. It is at rest because it is a rock and thus static. Its fissures, however, appear to be in motion like the eddies of water at play when tides go out and return to the bay. Such motion beckons the human spirit to delve into the mystery hidden from our sight beyond the narrow openings in the rock.

We find ourselves drawn to the paradox of a wall of rock which is both at rest and in motion. The crevice's illumination comes only from its entrance. Similarly, the openings in which we find ourselves can be dark. When we connect with the mystery beyond, moving deeper into darkness, we travel in hope. And we receive the gift of light only by journeying through such darkness.

By being drawn into the journey, we receive God's gift of a future. The light on the rock beckons us to future possibilities. We do not create the future. Rather we are given the future as a gift.

This truth can be difficult to accept. If we rely solely on our own resources, we risk not responding to God's grace-filled invitation into the future. We might cling to the security and protection of the fissures within the recesses of the rock, luminous or dark as they might be. Fissures, however, always have less light and safety than what we need and they can cause us to fall. We may be anxious about God's grace-filled invitation into the future. However, once this future is given and received, we venture no loss when we share those gifts we have to offer the world. The paradox is, as St. Francis put it, that in giving we receive, in dying we are reborn.

To venture, when invited by wonder, is to be exposed to the untested limits and unexplored boundaries of one's experience. If it is God who beckons us to walk through the darkness, then it is God who will hold us in his promise as we venture. With God, we are always more secure than we feel. Our anxiety is only the flipside of adventure. To be led by God's light is to be permitted to receive the future as gift.

God of Wonder, you are our rock and our salvation. Call us into the possibilities of the future and direct our journey with your loving Spirit. Let the brightness of your light illuminate our journey and dispel the darkness that sometimes overshadows the possibilities we encounter. Fill us with excitement about the future and guide our exploration of the mysteries that lie ahead. Let it be so.

Ephatha: Be Open

What does God tell us in a mountain shrouded in purple dusk? How does God speak through the color of royalty? What does the Creator, who crafts mountains and valleys, mean to say?

The Enlightenment philosopher, Johann Georg Hamann said, "God speaks to the creature through the creature." By the creature Hamann meant whatever God makes, such as planets, stars, mountains, valleys, plants, animals, and people. Hamann based that assertion on the incarnation. God has most clearly spoken to the world in a creature, the man Jesus Christ. In Jesus Christ, the creator God and the human creature are one.

All creation witnesses to the truth. Creation is God's address to us. Creation is God communicating to us. The Psalmist affirms, "The heavens are telling the glory of God; and the firmament proclaims his handiwork. Day to day pours forth speech, and night to night declares knowledge" (Psalm 19:1-2). What opens our ears so that we may listen? What opens our eyes that we might see? What delights would God give to us in a mountain shrouded in royal purple?

In this image, the royal God is speaking to us in power, steadfastness, and patience. Here God asserts that he is "our refuge and strength; the source of strength in times of trouble" (Psalm 46:2). God's message in creation is that we are given an Eden to enjoy, and this paradise will provide and sustain us together with all other creatures. How can we not but honor God for these treasures?

The sages of old affirmed, "The fear of the Lord is the beginning of wisdom" (Proverbs 1:7). Usually, we associate fear with something bad, shameful, or negative. Fear may often, however, be a very natural response for dealing with uncanny forces. We do well to have a healthy respect for this world. While the world seeps great joy, it is also taut with danger.

God is not lacking in spirit, zest, or the capacity to surprise, excite, or disarm us. In *The Chronicles of Narnia*, C. S. Lewis pictures Christ as Aslan, a powerful lion who, although committed to us, is not tame. Such is the power of God. God is not at our behest. We serve God, not in slavish fear, but with the appropriate respect that a child reserves for a trustworthy parent.

King of Glory, speak to us through the majesty and beauty of your creation. Fill our senses with awe and delight. Challenge us. Surprise us. Inspire us. Nurture us. Strengthen us. Empower us. Raise us up to be faithful stewards and witnesses of all that you have made. Let us be known as followers of your Son, Jesus Christ our Lord. Amen.

Mourning or Morning

We know that the whole creation has been groaning in labor pains until now; and not only the creation, but we ourselves, who have the first fruits of the Spirit, groan inwardly while we wait for adoption, the redemption of our bodies. (Romans 8:22-23)

I believe that God has created me together with all that exists. God has given me and still preserves my body and soul…—along with all the necessities and nourishment for this body and life. God protects me against all danger and shields and preserves me from all evil. And all this is done out of pure, fatherly, and divine goodness and mercy, without any merit or worthiness of mine at all for all of this I owe it to God to thank and praise, serve and obey him. This is most certainly true. *

Can impersonal nature be seen as personal? It can be personified, but not always easily. Surely, the image of creation as a woman experiencing the pain of childbirth stretches our imaginations.

St. Paul proclaims Christ not only as a personal Savior, but also as Lord of the cosmos. Martin Luther understood this Pauline truth. In the quotation above, he ties the language of God's creative activity to that of God's saving or justifying activity. The mention of human worthiness borrows language from the discussion of appropriate candidacy to the Lord's Table. The mention of merit takes language from the doctrine of justification. Surprisingly, for Luther, creation and salvation are not different things. Rather, grace liberates nature, restores creation. We might be so bold as to say that for Luther, God's creation is God's justification and vice versa.

All this invites us to explore our earthly existence. Given the centrality of the earth to created existence, we need to be vigilant with our use of the earth. All too often, we neglect the earth. We fail to be the caretakers of the precious garden of delight that God is planting. In pursuit of our perceived self-interest, we sacrifice the creation with technologies that foul the air, pollute the waters, and clear off the topsoil. The earth has been wounded by human sins.

Creation is groaning for redemption (Romans 8:18-25). In the new heavens and earth, there will be no more sorrow and no more tears. All these "former things" will pass away (Revelation 21-22).

The image, with its earth-like texture and almost monochromatic tones, is striking and startling. We can sense the eye of "mother earth" waiting in hope and effaced with tears. God will wipe away all tears, the tears of the persecuted, of the mourning, and even the tears from "mother earth."

Creation is what God has done, is doing, and will continue to do. Human neglect and self-centeredness will not stop God's goodness. The pain that hurts creation will come to an end. The human, bearing both the image of God and the humus of the earth, will likewise be set free of its self-centered violence. The "former things" will pass away.

And great will be that joy of resurrection morning!

---

*The Creed, the First Article, **The Book of Concord**, edited by Robert Kolb and Timothy J. Wengert, Minneapolis: Fortress Press, p. 354.

Creator God, keep your eye forever on us. Protect us from the evil that is around and within us. Stretch our imagination and strengthen our will. Empower us to claim the freedom that is ours as children of God. Let us rejoice, always, in the joy of Christ's and our resurrection. So be it.

Release

Life is a journey, a pilgrimage. How does that pilgrimage look when we are lost in panic? It is natural to be anxious. Anxiety is one way the creator helps creatures defend themselves from danger or motivates them to seek a more secure well-being.

When anxiety overwhelms you, however, it never secures the coveted well-being or protection that it desires. Instead, anxiety makes the journey frenetic, disjointed, and too intense for any kind of enjoyment. In short, anxiety and panic can be torture. To the degree that you are possessed by anxiety, the real person is kept submerged.

Anxiety can wear a variety of masks. However, the most deceptive faces of anxiety are those which are most socially acceptable, like feigning vulnerability so as to garner others' care-giving or feigning invulnerability so as to be unsociable.

For the anxious person, God is "too small," as J. B. Philips put it. Nevertheless, God loves the anxious person. If you the anxious person would live from that, you could gain a handle on your anxiety. Very often, God permits more in life than what the anxious person finds acceptable.

The philosopher Johann Georg Hamann pointed out that the true aesthetic before God is found in accepting one's status as a creature. It is to agree with that angel from The Book of Revelation who preaches the eternal gospel, "Fear God and give him the glory, for the hour of judgment has come; and worship him who made heaven and earth, the sea and the springs of water" (Revelation 14:7). The fear of God helps us put all other fears in perspective. It teaches us that God is at the center of reality and that from this truth our lives are always secure, whether we feel secure or not.

Panic is an illusion that God will not take care of us. But to live by faith is to let go of shouldering the weight of the world. Faith can accept that God provides, defends, and upholds. With God, we need not fight or flee things that threaten us. We can discover more creative options. With God, we are in the best hands.

With faith, our pilgrimage becomes an adventure, not merely a mechanical passing through life. Only with faith does life have meaning and hope. In short, wounds that we find unacceptable and from which we want to protect ourselves, God can and will use to clear any illusion that he, and he alone, will provide through all circumstances. Thus, we need to look beyond the guilt and shame that contributes to anxiety. God is making our lives to be not just bearable but exciting.

Beloved Savior, let the light of your love shatter the darkness that threatens to overpower us. Free us from the anxieties that accompany our earthly journey so that we may live our lives beyond anxiety. Help us to have faith that you give meaning to our lives. You guide our journey in life. You will finally lead us safely home. Amen.

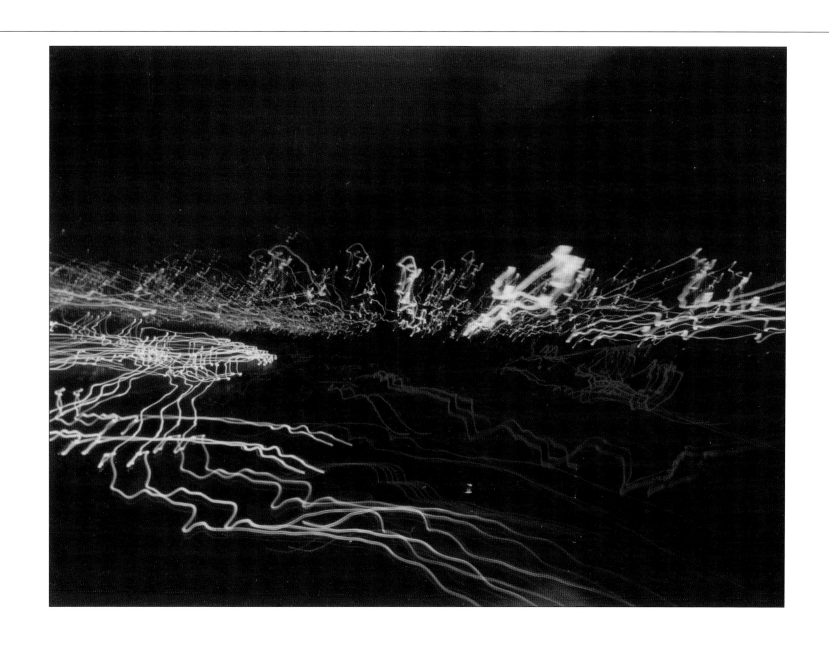

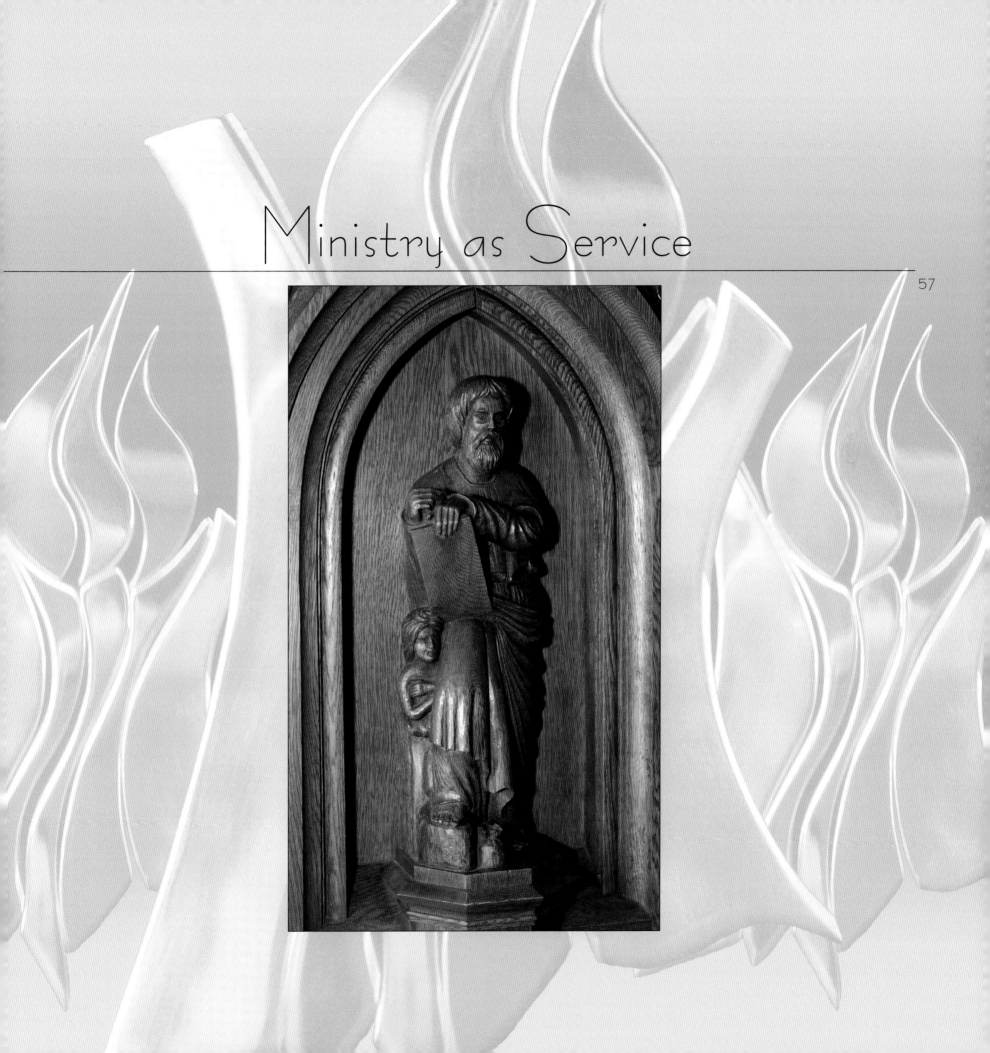

Temples

"Not in these temples made with hands, God the Most High is dwelling. High in the heavens his temples stand, all earthly temples excelling" (Lutheran Book of Worship, #161). In that hymn of the Danish educator and theologian, N. F. S. Grundtvig, we sing the truth that all human enterprises fall short of the majesty of the eternal God. God's dwelling place is the whole heavens and earth and not any human creation.

The hymn, like our image, raises the question of genuine worship. Surprisingly, worship is not primarily our action to God, but God's action to and for us. It is God's creative moment by moment self-giving to us. It is not first and foremost our sacrifice of praise, thanks, or earthly gifts. Rather, it is God who has sacrificed himself and continues to give of himself to sustain us. God's sacrifice is not just the gifts God gives in church. It is the gift of life itself. Because of it, the distinction between the sacred and the profane, or the spiritual and secular, is artificial. All things in this world reflect the sacredness of God, to some degree or another.

Some Christians make icons, not to have pictures, but to honor God's presence throughout the universe. God gives himself most clearly in Jesus Christ. Since Jesus Christ is fully human (as well as fully divine), God has bound himself to this cosmos of creaturely life. As people of faith, we share in Christ's continuing ministry in the world as we offer the good news, forgive sins, feed the hungry, visit the prisoner, care for one another, and render justice to the oppressed.

God is everywhere present and giving, but God is not everywhere present and giving *for us*. Many think they can worship God apart from church, on the golf course, for instance. The golf course, however, does not speak a word of forgiveness or mercy. Furthermore, the golf course is a place where lightning strikes. How can that assure us that God is for us?

In the church, we are granted the truth that God is for us. The altar is not a place of sacrifice, but of nourishment through bread and wine as the body and blood of Christ "given and shed for you for the forgiveness of sin." God invites us to it! We are always the invited one. God welcomes each sinner to this banquet. In the church, the Holy Spirit bathes us in the water of baptism and illuminates us through the scriptures. In the church, the pulpit is not a forum for personal opinions, but of testifying to God's requirements and delivering God's promise.

The church as sanctuary should be a safe place, an icon of God's love. In this icon, God reaches out to embrace, affirm, and make available his grace. In return, we acknowledge, "O how blessed is this place, filled with solace, light and grace" (*Lutheran Book of Worship*, #250).

Nowhere is the message of God's generosity more clear. Here we are safe and may now provide a refuge and ministry for others in the world.

How blessed are we, O God of the Universe, for your gift of creation and for your presence among us. We give thanks, especially, for your gift of the Church. Renew and strengthen its work among your people. Continue to nourish us with your presence in worship and in our daily lives. Let the radiance of the cross be a constant reminder of your love for us and an empowering symbol of your call to service. Amen.

Baptism

To see the full effect of a fountain, we must view it from a distance. To see the source of a fountain, however, we must move close to its center. In the turbulent texture of this image of water, eddies and flumes play among the swirling hues of red, blue, and yellow. For our purposes, this image represents holy baptism, whose regenerating power is given as love beaming out from Jesus Christ.

To move to the font, to the source, is to move to Jesus Christ, the heart of eternal life. He is victor over sin, death, the devil, and the accusing law. In him is the resurrection and the life. "In Holy Baptism our gracious heavenly Father liberates us from sin and death, joining us to the death and resurrection of our Lord Jesus Christ" (*Lutheran Book of Worship*, p. 121).

Water is one of the earth's primal elements, sustaining all living things. Water covers three-fourths of the earth's surface. The human body is 90% water. In the waters and Word of baptism, we are given more than a name. We are given God's commitment that our lives are sealed in his love. Our old being dies with Christ and we are reborn.

Water cleanses. Through water and the Word, we are cleansed and blessed with new life. In baptism, we receive God's love and forgiveness. Forgiven, we can forgive. Baptism takes human plurality and honors it by enfolding it into the rich diversity of the one church, the "mother of Christians." "By water and the Holy Spirit we are made members of the church which is the body of Christ."

In the life of the church, we are many. In baptism, however, we share a common story and identity in Christ. God's pool and people are never stagnant. They are alive, active, fresh, and free-flowing. Jesus tells us that "whoever believes in him living waters will flow forth from him" (John 7:37-39).

O God, the Giver of Life, pour out upon us your Holy Spirit. Liberate us from the sinful thoughts and deeds of the past and renew us with your life-giving love. Cleanse and bless us with new life. In Baptism, we were marked with the sign of the cross forever. Help us to live out our lives in the fullness of that gift as members of the body of Christ and as "inheritors of eternal life." Amen.

The Integrity of Ministry

St. Paul writes, "But how are they to call on the one in whom they have not believed? And how are they to believe in one of whom they have never heard? And how are they to hear without someone to proclaim him? And how are they to proclaim him unless they are sent?" (Romans 10:14-15).

It is on record that within the last several decades the public confidence in clergy has significantly decreased. At one time, clergy belonged to one of the most trusted of professions. That does not seem to be the case today.

Are clergy responsible, to some degree, for their loss of prestige? Are clergy responsible, to some degree, for promoting people for the pastoral office who are unable to deliver trust?

We Americans want to identify with a charismatic figure as our ideal pastor. We project our ideals onto such a figure and presume that we have someone who understands us and with whom we can personally identify.

The notion that the clergy belong to the office of Word and Sacrament must sound cold and impersonal. Is it not true, however, that the current loss of prestige among the clergy is due, significantly, to the fact that we lack people in this office whose character traits match the requirements of the office? We need people of integrity to proclaim earnestly God's message.

Not the warmth of the minister's personality, but the integrity of how one conducts one's office is what can restore confidence in ministry.

Ministry is ambassadorial. In the pulpit, one is not to share especially one's political opinions or personal idiosyncrasies. Instead, one is an *angelos*, an angel, a messenger.

There is very little that is sentimental about angels as presented in the Bible. Usually when they arrive, they have to say, "Fear not!" because their very presence startles, even terrifies, those they address.

All things in the world convey God's message; however, not all things convey God's message of mercy with clarity. Here the preaching office is that angelic office which imparts God's mercy, comfort, and forgiveness. There is a formality here from which we ought not to disassociate ourselves.

A blessing is bestowed in the very words of benediction. Forgiveness is granted in the very words of absolution. The office that conveys this should not be undermined.

Pastors who are able to exercise the office that sustains them hold themselves accountable to the public integrity that the ministerial office needs today.

Pastors dare not forget whom they represent. They are ambassadors of Christ!

Anointed One, raise up from our midst faithful servants of integrity and stewards of your Word and Sacraments. Help us to receive these servants as heralds of your saving grace. Strengthen, also, the efforts of all faithful people everywhere to encourage and to pray for these messengers as we, together, seek to proclaim the Good News that liberates creation for new life and service. Amen.

The Preacher

Almighty God, you chose the Virgin Mary to be the mother of your only Son. Grant that we, who have been redeemed by his blood, may share with her in the glory of your eternal kingdom; through your Son, Jesus Christ our Lord, who lives and reigns with you and the Holy Spirit one God, now and forever. (Lutheran Book of Worship, p. 34)

Mary is the mother of Jesus Christ. How does she want to be honored or remembered?

She makes it very clear. Mary is primarily a preacher. She is one of the best. Her "sermon," commonly known as The *Magnificat*, speaks clearly:

My soul magnifies the Lord,
and my spirit rejoices in God my Savior,
For he has regarded the low estate of his
　　handmaiden.

For behold, henceforth all generations will
　　Call me blessed;
for he who is mighty has done great
　　things for me,
　　and holy is his name.

And his mercy is on those who
　　fear him
　　from generation to generation

He has shown strength with his
arm,

he has scattered the proud in the imagination of their hearts,
he has put down the mighty from their thrones,
and exalted those of low degree;

he has filled the hungry with good
　　things,
and the rich he has sent empty
　　away.

He has helped his servant, Israel,
in remembrance of his mercy,
as he spoke to our fathers,
to Abraham and to his posterity
　　for ever.
　　(Luke 1:46-55)

Mary's song testifies to God's mercy: "For the Mighty One has done great things for me, and holy is his name. His mercy is for those who fear him...."

Even though Mary has a royal lineage, she was born poor. She could have complained about her lack of status and wealth, but that was not her way. Instead, at the invitation to mother the Savior, her response was one of gratitude.

She knew the social dynamics between the "haves" and the "have-nots."

More importantly, she knew God's position towards the poor. "He has brought down the powerful from their thrones, and lifted up the lowly; he has filled the hungry with good things, and sent the rich away empty" (Luke 1:52-53). Mary understood how unfair life can be. She also understood that everything in life is a gift.

Like Mary, before God, we can earn nothing. Before a holy God, we deserve even less. Yet, God gives everything. So how can we not serve God and our neighbor? That truth Mary understood. God is the giver of good gifts. We are offered them and strengthened for service to our neighbor.

"...my soul magnifies the Lord, and my spirit rejoices in God my Savior, for he looked with favor on the lowliness of his servant" (Luke 1:46-48).

Mighty One, let us rejoice, as did Mary the Mother of our Lord, in your boundless generosity and mercy. Fill our hearts with gratitude for the "great things" you have done for us. Let us not forget, however, those in our society who are in need. Direct our attention and acts of service to their care. May we all magnify the Lord for his continuing favor. Amen.

Authority for Service

The uncertainties of life do not deter us from continually seeking the means to live life to its fullest. The tree in the center of the image appears to be the strongest element in the composition. Appearances can be deceiving. Remember the illustration: you can break a single twig easily, but many twigs combined are not easily broken. The tree is but a support for the vine, which possesses its own creative power. The power in the vine is manifest in its circular motion, giving life to the entire image. Its strength is found in its creativity for growth which gives it motion and unity.

In the circling of the vine about the tree, new life is indicated. According to the gospel of John, Jesus Christ is the vine and we are the branches (John 15:5). He is the source of our life. Our union in him is not found in imitating his ethical directives. Nor is it found in mystical transformation. Rather, our union in Christ is found in God's claim, "you belong to me" in Jesus Christ. God's word says what it does and does what it says. Jesus' resurrection eliminates all other claimants over us. God is so *for us* that he *becomes one with us* and makes us to be one with him.

This claim is administered to us in a baptismal washing and a consecrated meal. God makes good on his claim by reconciling us in baptismal water and feeding us through sacramental bread and wine. Sin, death, and the devil have no rights over us. God's claim prevails over every contender. In this claim, God restores us to creation as it is intended to be. We are one with God as a child is bonded to a parent. Thus, we do not even own ourselves. God owns us, and in his care we can see the world with new eyes.

The circular motion of the vine symbolizes the tip of a shepherd's staff. Its strength is found in the union of the branches whose shape and identity is from the vine. Where the church is, there is an overseer whose purpose is leadership among the faithful and who is accountable to the Shepherd. As shepherds under the Shepherd, pastors need to be vigilant with respect to integrity and accountability. Often, our instinct is to resist any authority or accountability. Spiritual overseers, however, need to claim authority to help people author their own lives in the life of the Good Shepherd. The strength of faithful pastoral leadership, and its authority, is mandated by the risen Lord: "Go into all the world…" (Matthew 28).

Beyond the vine, and its branches, is the rest of the world, here symbolized by a more distant background under a winter blue sky. It is Advent—blue—a season of hope for all. God is making good on his promise, "You are mine."

What appears to be strong is not always so, and what appears to be weak can indeed be strong. Our daily strength is in God's commitment to us, imparted through the church in Word and Sacrament, which is empowering us for ministry and service in the world.

Gentle Shepherd, you are our hope and our salvation. At baptism you marked us with the sign of the cross and claimed us as your own. You continue to nourish us with your word and the sacraments. May our union in you strengthen us for service this day and in the days to come. Amen.

Accountability of Ministry

Receive this stole as a sign of your work, and walk in obedience to the Lord Jesus, serving his people and remembering his promise: "Come to me, all who labor and are heavy laden, and I will give you rest. Take my yoke upon you, and learn from me; for I am gentle and lowly in heart, and you will find rest for your souls. For my yoke is easy, and my burden is light." (Matthew 11:28-30)

Care for God's people, bear the burdens and do not betray their confidence. So discipline *yourself* in life and teaching that you preserve the truth, giving no occasion for false security or illusory hope. Witness faithfully in word and deed to all people. Give and receive comfort as you serve within the Church. And be of good courage, for God has called you, and your labor is not in vain.*

This is how one should regard us, as servants of Christ and stewards of the mysteries of God. Moreover it is required of stewards that they be found trustworthy (1Corinthians 4:1-2).

How does God listen to our joys and our sorrows, and relieve and heal us? We sometimes assume that access to God is direct and immediate, a matter of going into one's heart. In that view, no pastor, priest, or intermediary is needed.

We are wrong. After all, Jesus Christ is the go-between between God and people. God only speaks through others, even when that other is Balaam's donkey. Most clearly, God speaks through the scriptures. God's speech plucks out our sin and builds us up in faith.

It is God who descends to us, not we who ascend to God. God's advent to us is always given through means, in baptismal water, sacramental bread and wine, and the pastor's voice as the penitent is forgiven. Christ upholds the one who is called to engage in the priestly task of hearing confession. To hear confession is to offer the very ear of Christ.

To hear confession, however, is not always to forgive. In fact, there are two keys: one for loosing the sins of the penitent and the other for binding the sins of the impenitent. Both are offered out of mercy. When sins are not forgiven, it is a warning to provoke repentance and amendment of life.

The power to loose and to bind the conscience is a sacred service. Any person entrusted with such power must take this charge seriously and earnestly. At its best, pastoral power will build up a community. All persons are called to share that task. A pastor's focus should be to nurture Christian community through the Word of God and the life-giving sacraments.

*(Ordination in *Occasional Services*, Minneapolis: Augsburg Publishing House and Board of Publication, Lutheran Church in America, 1982, p. 197)

Beloved Master, you have called each of us to service in this world. Prepare our hearts to receive that call with humility and devotion. Speak to us through the Church and through the words and deeds of your people. Make us faithful stewards of the mysteries that belong to you alone. Amen.

The Beauty of Healthy Community

The image is fragile! The image is intense in shapes, patterns, textures, and colors! A deep blue inverted heart shape is born within a turquoise circle. The circle, in turn, is sustained in a brownish acorn shape surrounded in yellow with a black color stretching outward like a translucent halo. The intensity and contrast of the colors are enlarged by each other, achieving a balance and harmony, beyond the color-code.

The shapes, patterns, textures, and colors cohere through the convergence of vanes growing in increasing unanimity along the shaft of the image. Vanes, colors, shapes, and shaft combine to form a complex but simple infrastructure. The inviting message of the dark blue core is offered because of the diverse vanes that move toward togetherness. In all their plurality and diversity, they join as one common voice, offering a unity like a baroque fugue, with repetitions of common patterns and themes. The common life of each vane with the other does not detract, but adds to the diversity and unity of the whole. In this way, their individuality is fulfilled in addition to the whole.

Human life is intense. Human life is fragile. Human life can be fragmented in the individual and in the faith community. However, this is no reason to neglect the quest for healthy community. Healthy community augments the life of the individual. It can put fragility and fragmentation into perspective. The distortions resulting from brokenness and fragmentation offer possibilities and promises of new life when channeled into fairness and mutual governance. Apart from the main shaft, the beauty of the vanes cannot be sustained. Apart from mutual leadership seeking good order, a community of faith cannot use its power for service in the world.

So, then, the question is: what beauty might healthy human community offer?

All too often a person or community of faith takes life for granted. Individuals and communities ignore the accountability of our gifts as they contribute to the common good.

How do I wish to share my gift and power in the community of faith?

How do I seek to build up the body of Christ for mission in the world? To whom can I look for growth in faith and life? How do I mentor others? Answers to these questions and others will be provided when we intentionally ask them.

God seeks to foster and enrich a unity that blossoms with the prospect of greater diversity, many voices in a shared vision.

We give you thanks, Lord of All, for the gift of community and for the many and varied communities which enrich our lives. For our families and loved ones, for our colleagues and neighbors, and for the members of our communities of faith, we are grateful. May these communities strengthen our faith in you and empower us for the ministry you call us to do. Amen.

Conflict

Nothing seems to invite emotional tranquility more than the perpetual motion of a body of water. Here a lake, surrounded by mountains, would seem to provide and welcome such serenity.

Brooding above the highest peaks, however, is an ominous cloud. Is it rain just over the horizon? Standing at the shoreline, our sense of smell provides the answer. It is not rain, but a cloud of thick smoke, the product of a forest fire. We cannot see the fire…yet! But, we can see, feel, and taste its product of heavy, thick, black, choking smoke.

In nature, a forest fire is a natural event, as natural as the line of evergreens on the lakeshore across from us. And, the fire is deadly. It destroys everything in its path. We can almost touch the on-coming cloud pushing closer from the horizon.

Similarly, church leaders are often quite good at discerning clouds of anxiety within a faith community. Like the forest fire, the signs are visible: rudeness, a lack of boundaries, and a mean-spirited presence. When such anxieties get out of hand, they can be every bit as destructive as a forest fire to its inhabitants.

God has high ambitions for human community. God wills human community to be one of respect, integrity, and peace. However, anxiety within a community can often get the upper hand and the community falls short of the goal of this desired respect, integrity, and peace.

Where there are people, there will be differences. Unfortunately, self-sabotaging behaviors seem to be just as human as self-enhancing ones. As a result, human communities, like individuals, are capable of neurotic behavior. Like individuals, communities can get their own stomach-aches, headaches, and muscle spasms.

Conflict cannot be avoided, but it can be dealt with when people are willing to challenge those tactics which hurt others and demean the perpetrator as well.

It is easy to deceive ourselves into thinking that conflict happens only to others. Conflict is common in a sinful world. Every leader should be prepared to deal with conflict. Leaders should hold up the common good as a standard by which to challenge aggression.

Leaders need to handle adversity in ways that will lead the community to a more effective level of mission. This they can do by modeling a life of respect, integrity, and peace.

Our Lord Jesus, open our hearts to the goodness that you have created in each of us. Guide our actions and our words by your command to love one another. Where there is conflict, empower us to constructively challenge those tactics and attitudes which are destructive to the wholeness and unity that you desire for us. Help us to model lives of respect, integrity, and peace. Amen.

Conflict Endured

In this image we see the effects and magnitude of the forest fire. Smoke engulfs the mountains and shadows the lake. Breathing, for humans and animals alike, becomes more challenging. The July sun struggles to shine through the darkness. Indeed, darkness begins to settle over the land at four in the afternoon. Fighting a forest fire demands discipline and boundaries if all the fire fighters are to bring the fire under control.

Sometimes, change within a community can create darkness and conflict for both membership and leadership. We delude ourselves if we think that conflict is not a part of a congregation's growth and ministry. Adolescents often struggle with themselves as they grow. Congregations do too, if they are to grow.

Conflict is not all bad. What matters is how we respond to it. It can be an invitation for growth in communication skills, improvement of social skills, and in basic understanding.

Ministry in communities of faith engages adversity at all levels in life. We can hardly think of any of the great leaders in scripture, such as Moses, David, the prophets, Paul, and our Lord himself, apart from encountering adversity and conflict. They all grew as a result of conflict. Indeed, much of their ministry was leading people through conflict that the people either themselves generated or received from others.

The test of leadership is how conflict is handled. Does it evoke blame so that people can invoke the status of victim? Or does conflict evoke creative responsibility for oneself and the care of others? Leaders sometimes choose to see themselves as victims, especially when they make others' anxiety their own. Still other leaders neglect or fail to establish appropriate boundaries. Such boundaries could help establish a more workable approach to problem solving. Indeed, neglect of boundaries simply ends up feeding conflict.

Like dealing with a forest fire, good ministry in a faith community during times of conflict requires discipline and boundaries to deal with differences successfully. One of the most important questions to ask, before, during, and after conflict is: what can be done to generate as much health as possible in the situation for people to proceed?

Major conflict will never be allayed in all life situations. Nonetheless, focusing on the question of generating the best health possible is a foundation that provides a beginning that will produce some surprising, creative directions.

Merciful God, give us the courage and strength to meet the challenges that we encounter in our daily lives. In moments of adversity, let your light shine through the darkness that sometimes clouds our vision and our hope. Help us to resist the temptation to assign blame or to seek retaliation when we are disappointed. May your peace be always with us. Amen.

Moving Beyond Conflict

Smoke now covers the land. It obliterates any vision beyond the most immediate, yet, we are preserved from the fire. Of course, not everything is preserved, for much of the forest is destroyed and its animal inhabitants scattered. Such destruction saddens us, but it seems to be the way with nature.

Despite this devastation, after the fire, there is new life that will appear in the following spring. From death and destruction, new life emerges.

We do not always anticipate the new life that comes from the violence and conflict in communities. During times of adverse conflict, it seems that nothing good can result from it.

In this final picture of our trilogy of forest fire images, smoke darkens the sky, over the forest and even the lake, almost absolutely. But please look carefully, again! The sun remains. The smoke does not eradicate the light of nature's sun completely.

That is like hope. Hope sustains us in the midst of conflict. Hope is not only for survival or to cope with turmoil. Instead, hope is for a better world, a better life, and a better community. Hope calls us to believe that problems will be worked through so that they will never take hold of us again in the same way. Hope claims that leaders grow in their ability to discern the signs that may bring hurt to the community and have proper skills to deal with violence.

It is important that leaders, in any community, are aware how their fears contribute to or invite conflict to develop. Leaders need to ask, "What can be learned from this experience? How can I grow because of it? How can I become more effective?" Together, all will discover how conflict can become an opportunity for better ministry in the days ahead. That takes courage in the largest sense.

Ultimately, faith believes that God is at work in all things to sustain, nurture, and help us grow throughout life. Hope, for its part, believes that God will make good on the promise of a new heaven and earth.

The forest fire will ultimately diminish and go out when it has nothing left to consume, along with good fire-fighting attention. All violence feeds off goodness. All sickness lives off health. There is no guarantee of a conflict-free world.

As noted, the other side of anxiety is adventure. To lead effectively through and beyond conflict is an adventure in hope facing up to and facing down conflict and sickness within a community. Winning or losing in the adventure is not our call to make, for finally life is not our game. We are instead enclosed in the hands of a God who will not fail. Ours is a discipleship, a calling faithful in service, shaped by the cross. The resurrection is already assured.

Dearest Jesus, pour out upon us your forgiving grace and draw us together as your people. Help us to see new opportunities amidst the disappointments and trials of our daily lives. Call us into the adventure of new life in you, a life beyond conflict and adversity, a life of faithful discipleship and service. Let it be so.

Affirming the Other

In the photographic image, we see a vivid red backdrop and a cool blue agent. The colors indicate a contrast between heat and coolness. It would appear that the blue agent is entering the red field. In actuality, that is too simplistic a view. The blue agent enters, and thereby it meets both reception and resistance. It not only acts but is acted upon. The red field has an agency of its own. The blue agent alters the terrain of the red horizon, but it also receives polishing from the red horizon, which heightens its very blueness. The field's redness brings the agent's blueness to the fore while the blue object likewise highlights the redness.

What is the nature of the blue object's entrance? Is its entrance smooth or rough? To all appearances it is smooth. In truth, however, this might be the result of the agency of the red field over time, taking disruptive, rough edges away from it. The blue object and the red field have each worked upon the other. Thereby both the blue agent and the red field complement each other. Each has something to bring to the other. They each accentuate the other's strengths, help shore up each other's weaknesses, and thus both become life-affirming for each other.

Life has interruptions, intrusions, and even violations. We encounter the other in many different ways. Whether perceived as friend or foe, the other bids for our attention. Christ commands us to "love one another." We are called to love even our enemies.

This is counter-intuitive. When we are wronged, we want to even the score. We intend thereby to affirm our dignity. Revenge, however, comes at a cost. Hatred feeds more hatred and even self-hatred. With revenge, we never find the healing of Christ's love.

Theologian Harold Ditmanson pointed out that God's grace helps us affirm life rather than regard it with fear or contempt. To hold on to hatred is to hold life in contempt.

We are forgiven in Jesus Christ. Forgiven, we can forgive. Affirmation of life and the other comes from a heart full of God's loving kindness that trumps the desire for one-upmanship or revenge. Forgiveness means more than to ignore or overlook. Those ploys fail to quell violence. Forgiveness means to wish goodness on the other, even one's enemy.

Just as the blue agent and the red field accentuate each other, the other has a place in one's life. Whether friend or foe, the other is God's instrument, pushing and pulling me, through which God crafts me. I, likewise, am God's instrument through which that other is crafted. Martin Luther called this relational dynamic God "masking" himself in nature and others. In God's embrace, my strengths and my weaknesses find their place. This is true for the other as well. In God's creation our lives are intertwined and serve towards growth and enrichment. In this way, we can affirm with Paul, "All things work together for good to those who love God, who are called according to his purpose" (Romans 8:28).

Living God, you know our comings and our goings; our strengths and our weaknesses; our differences and our similarities. Let our strength be in our diversity and our unity in our love for you and the affirmation of one another. Open our hearts to your grace and bind us together. Amen.

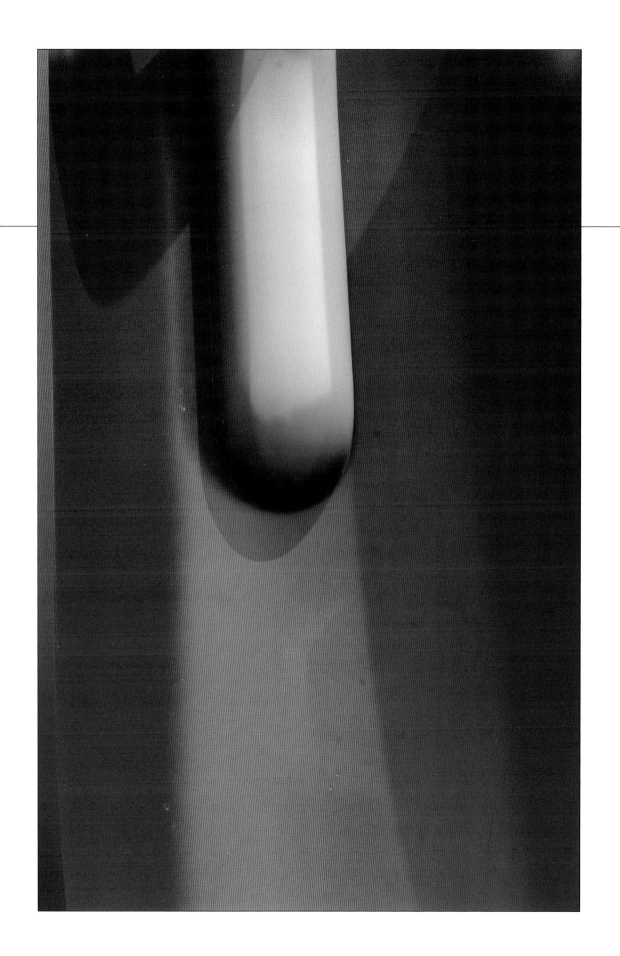

Vocation

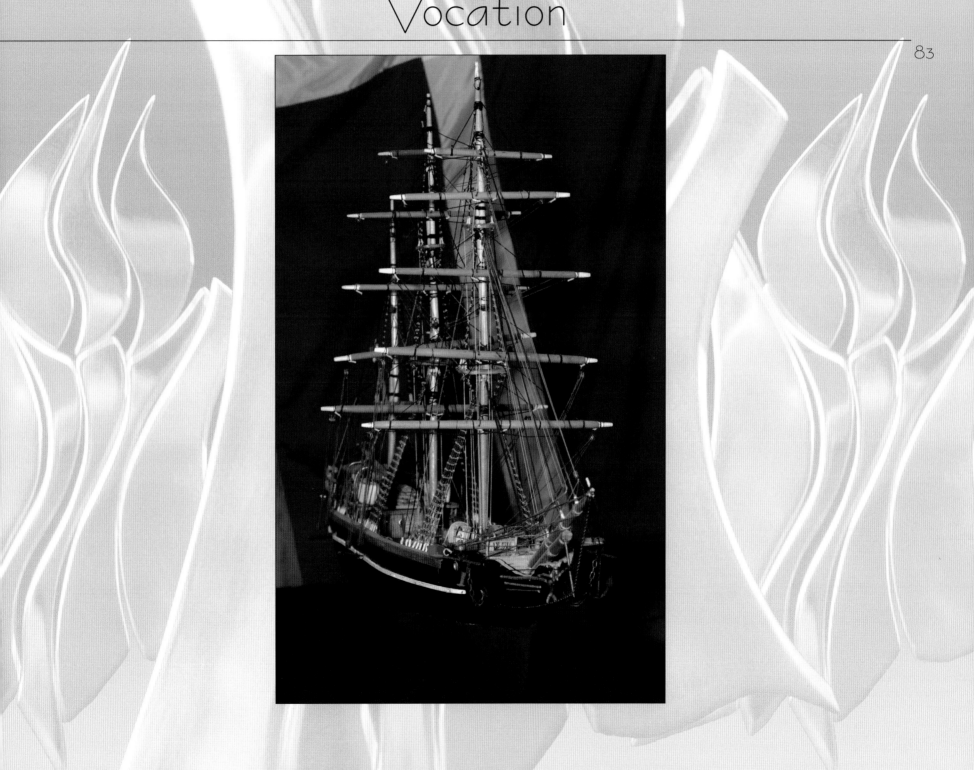

Partnering

The Lord God in his goodness created us male and female, and by the gift of marriage founded human community in a joy that begins now and is brought to perfection in the life to come. Because of sin, our age-old rebellion, the gladness of marriage can be overcast and the gift of the family can become a burden. But because God, who established marriage, continues still to bless it with his abundant and ever-present support, we can be sustained in our weariness and have our joy restored.*

Partnering has always brought its challenges. Conflict is a crucial and unavoidable part of cooperation. We simply do not always agree—that is good. The only way to move beyond disagreement is by means of discussion. As Roman Catholic theologian David Tracy teaches, argument is but a moment within conversation. Led by integrity, we honor our relationship to each other, not our self-pride, as primary. Overall, discussion helps us mutually offer insights that can move the relationship forward.

In the past, partnering was crucial to survival. Prior to the widespread use of technology, the members of farm families needed each other to help with planting, harvesting, and daily chores. Today, it appears we are more independent of each other. We live in neighborhoods where we often do not know our neighbors. We work in cubicles that seem even more impersonal.

Nevertheless, we are far more interdependent on each other than we recognize. The fact that we have never met the farmers who have raised our daily bread does not mean that we have no connection to them. Quite the opposite is true. Even in such anonymity we are dependent on their good graces and sense of responsibility.

Partnering continues to be important, indeed, vital. In partnering our strengths are augmented. In partnering, we share sufferings and blessings together. In partnering, we are able, as St. Paul

puts it to "rejoice with those who rejoice and weep with those who weep" (Romans 12:15). Individualism needs to be countered with the truth that I do not lose but rather gain myself through connecting with others—even through dependency—on others. Partnering does not lessen my identity but expands it through mutual interaction.

Marriage is a God-given, intimate form of partnering. It provides a special relationship for creative growth between male and female, the raising of a family, and the nurturing of intimacy, mutual support, solace, and joy. Marriage will never be problem-free. It has an important task in the school for character development. It can help persons cultivate their ability to grow in their fidelity to their word, to support and uphold one another in times of great joy and through deepest sorrows.

"It is not good for the man to be alone" (Genesis 2:7). We were meant for community and partnership. Thereby God works upon us crafting us to be the people God wants us to become.

---

*(Lutheran Book of Worship, p. 202.)

Lord Jesus, you created us and set us apart from other creatures to love and care for one another and to experience the joy of human community. It is through our relationships with one another that we come to know you more deeply and serve you more fully. Grant us friends and loved ones to comfort us in times of trial and to celebrate with us in times of joy. Give us gentle and compassionate companions to care for us and to carry out the work of your kingdom. Amen.

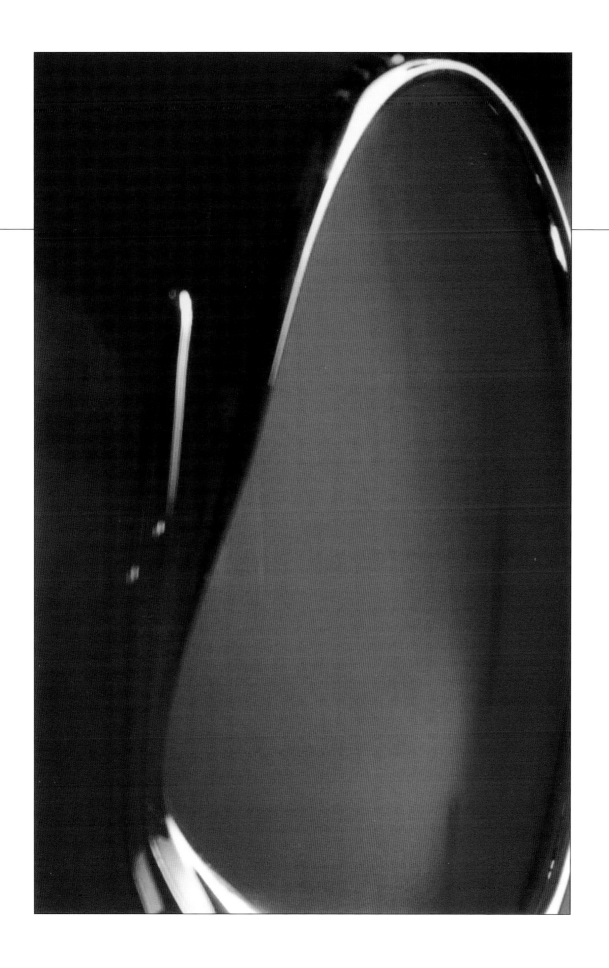

The Role of Government

At one time, it was a truism that although we are in the world, we are not of the world. This conviction needs to be reclaimed.

Christians are in the world. There is no doubt about that. Insofar as they also anticipate and live from God's coming world, however, they are not of the world.

Government is a this-worldly matter. As belonging to two realms, Christians have a mixed relationship with government. In a democracy, we are granted participation in government. However, Christians are painfully aware of the limitations of democracy in light of human sinfulness and God's goals for the world.

No doubt government can only do so much. Each citizen needs to contribute if the world is to become a better place.

Christians have an insight about government that some others may lack. It is that people can be idolatrous about their government. Belonging to two realms, Christians acknowledge that God's coming world is ultimate and that this world is penultimate. Consequently, this perspective makes the claims of government relative to those of God's kingdom.

Apart from faith, civil community itself becomes a kind of church with symbols that seek to bear an ultimate status. Since the government has the power both to take life and legislate war, it is not surprising that people come to regard it as sacred. That move, however, makes it all the more difficult to separate religion from politics, which we purportedly wish to do in our democracy. Ultimate matters should always be decided by an appeal to an ultimate reality. It's spurious to think the government can do that.

There may indeed be no state church in the United States, but there seems to be a kind of state-sanctioned religion: "civil religion," as sociologist Robert Bellah describes it. Otherwise, we would have no "ultimate" authority to which to appeal, especially in times of crises, defense, or for legitimating public policy.

While the government might appeal to some purported "ultimate" in order to sanction its goals, we Christians must hold it accountable to the Ultimate. If government arrogates power to itself that becomes self-deifying, then Christians must oppose such government as idolatrous. The most important reminder that Christians can give the government is the first commandment: "you shall have no other gods before me" (Exodus 20:3). When government seeks to serve people, Christians can and should affirm such a role.

We live in two kingdoms—two spheres of God's agency—God's governance through the state and God's governance through the church. God redeems life in the church. And God creates lives in the earthly orders of family and society. This latter sphere includes worldly politics. For Luther, worldly government is a result of the fall into sin. To share in the tasks of both on-going realms is healthy. To believe that somehow politics could save the world is unhealthy. Only God can save.

To fear, love, and trust in God above all things puts all of life into perspective. When our ultimate loyalties are properly ordered and balanced, then all penultimate matters, such as governmental affairs, are unleashed for service in the world

---

Gracious God, we pray this day for all who hunger for your love and justice. Call us each to greater service for the common good and strengthen our efforts to honor the responsibilities that are ours as members of your family—to care for one another and to pray for those who have been charged to labor in our behalf. Let us trust in you above all things. Amen.

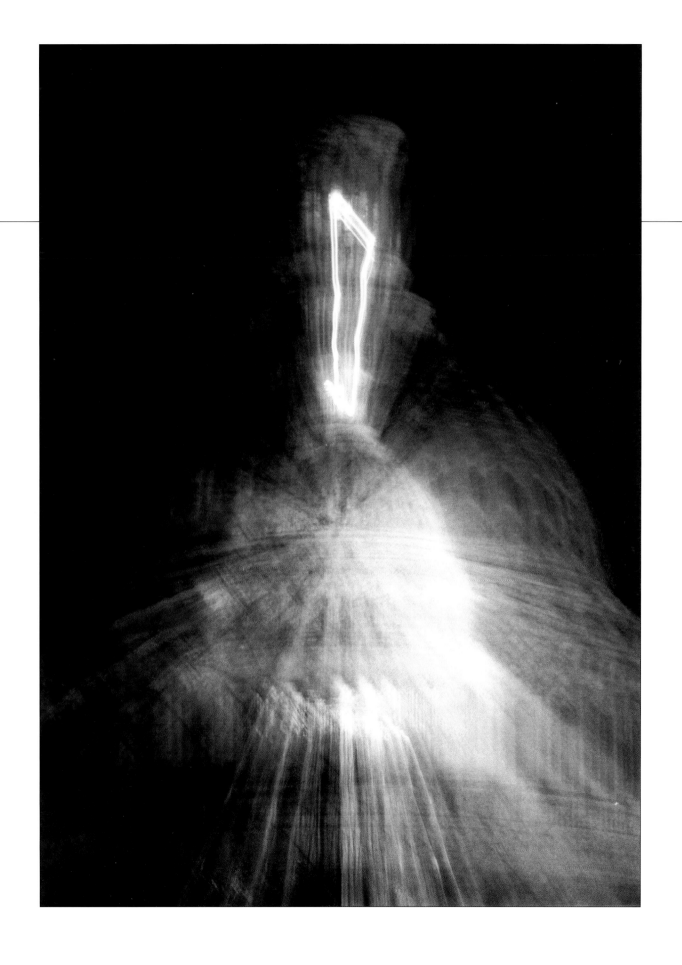

Building Bridges

88

The Psalmist wrote, "Unless the Lord builds the house they labor in vain who build it" (Psalm 127:1). God is doing the labor, building, reconstructing, all the time. If nothing else, that should give us permission to lighten our load. We make. God creates. We cannot make unless God creates. With God in charge, we are responsible for our vocations. And because we are not responsible for everything, that is good news.

God's work is building bridges. For the person of faith, God's coming in the flesh and life of Jesus is nothing other than a bridge between eternity and time, and between righteousness and sin. In Jesus Christ, both creator and creature are one. God's path to us is not a two-way street. The vertical bridge between God and the world goes in only one direction: down, down to us, and to the depths of our sin and brokenness.

God's righteousness claiming us makes us secure at our core. Faith means that we allow God to do his work in us. We suffer God, one might say. With respect to ultimate matters, our attempt to take charge and be in control are crushed, even demolished. Thereby we live a "receptive life" and experience a passive righteousness.

The counterpart to such passivity before God is our active, energetic engagement in the world. A bridge has been opened to us and with it we can open connections to others. A river, when a bridge is built across it, becomes an artificial barrier. Differences that may have divided peoples because of a "natural" boundary are revitalized.

In Des Moines, Iowa, the Des Moines River divides the city on the East from the city on the West. Historically, East-siders tended to be working class and blue collar. West-siders have tended to be professionals and white collar. These were artificial divisions dictated because of the economy. Christ does not acknowledge such divisions. Christ is the bridge between peoples. Those on both sides of the river can have the "riches of Christ" (Ephesians 3:8). This true wealth challenges our social distinctions on the basis of "merit." Only God can establish true worth. No one else can do that for us. Through the eyes of faith, such social, economic or other divisions are wholly artificial.

God has claimed us as his own from all evils. God brings new life. Our vocation is one of reclamation. We share a message of promise in a community that reclaims people from violence, abuse, defeat, victimization, and marginalization. The message is perpetually an Easter message. God raises the dead! The lost are found. Those who were dead are alive again!

Draw us together, dear Lord, so that your work within and through us might be accomplished. Break down the barriers that divide us and unite us in our love toward you and toward one another. Let us be known as bridge builders and peacemakers in our time. Make us one in you. Amen.

Let Peace Dance

Life bears a surplus of energy, whether we know it or not. We can see this in the fact that human understanding can be supplanted and increased by further understandings. The more we learn the more there is to learn. As Roman Catholic theologian Karl Rahner put it, we "swim in a sea of infinite mystery." In such excess, one can, consciously or unconsciously, celebrate the riches of life.

Peace is sometimes in great abundance and sometimes it is scarce. Between the boundaries of abundance or scarcity, how does peace celebrate life? How does peace dance? Peace dances when we are absorbed into a social fabric far wider than our own individual lives. In this image, color, variety, and symbolic pageantry swirl around and beyond us, permitting us to share a space that is both ours and not ours.

To dance is to celebrate life itself as art. To dance is to unite the social, the natural, and the symbolic into one. It is natural for humans, as social, symbolic creatures, to do this.

Peace is not the absence of adversity or war. Nor is peace perpetual, inner tranquility. Rather, peace as a human product is the quest for and establishment of personal and social health in the midst of adversity, war, or inner turmoil. The outcome of our quest is not possible until we are liberated from our foolish attempts to secure our own personal or social destiny. Letting God be God in our lives grants the peace that liberates the quest for peace. Jesus said, "My peace I give you, not as the world gives, give I unto you" (John 14:27).

In contrast, violence feeds off victims, scapegoats, and insecurity. Violence feeds more violence. It is never overcome by social engineering. Rather, violence can only be extinguished when new life is granted. New life is one with the surplus energy that God is weaving into the fabric of the cosmos.

To dance is to be in balance with the creation. At that point, both we and the creation can dance together. The planets in the skies waltz around the sun. The dandelions sway in the breeze and share their pungent odors. Are we really that different from the stars given that the building block of life, carbon, was baked in their core? An older generation may remember strictures against dancing. Such scruples ignore that the best way to praise the creator may be through dancing, as David did when he brought the Ark of the Covenant into Jerusalem.

"Weeping endures but a night; joy comes in the morning" (Psalm 30:5). To experience joy is to share in the excess wherewith God creates. From the perspective of joy, even our tears are creative.

God creates the diversities of people and cultures. There are no heathens to God, only redeemed children. With all God's children, peace can dance because God is restoring, renewing, and reconciling the whole creation from the self-centeredness that binds it. Thus, we can dance because we can share in the common movement of God's excessive, creative energy. Let the dance begin.

God of peace and tranquility, fill our hearts and restore our bodies with the peace that comes from faith in you. Help us, amid the busyness of our lives, to grow in our appreciation and our celebration of that gift of peace—a peace that gives birth to new life in you and in our relationships with one another. Let your peace be our guide today and always. Amen.

No More Walls

St. Paul wrote, "But now in Christ Jesus you who once were far off have been brought near by the blood of Christ. For he is our peace; in his flesh he made both groups (Jews and Gentiles) into one and has broken down the dividing wall, that is, the hostility between us" (Ephesians 2:14-15).

Does God break down all walls? Don't we need some walls for protection? Aren't some walls to be honored? In the Old Testament, the sacred space of the temple was reserved for the Jewish community alone. At one time, that reservation was deemed vital. It was a mark of privilege for God's chosen people in distinction to others. Notices proclaimed that the Gentiles who trespassed those walls did so on pain of death. In contrast, Paul reminds us that God's ministry in Jesus Christ reaches out to all. In Jesus' resurrected body, which bore human rejection and suffered violence, God breaks down walls that separate. Jesus Christ is God's reconciliation, God's peace, for the world. He makes the "dividing wall" of the ancient temple artificial and blind.

Note well who it is who makes for peace. It is God who provides peace, *shalom*. Liberated from sin, and for the good of creation, we cooperate with God's renewing energy. Our synergy, however, is effective only when partnering with God's task of restoring creation. We do not redeem the world. God redeems the world. God breaks down artificial walls and barriers. Walls, however, that protect us by establishing healthy boundaries rest on faith in God's reconciling action. If we give ourselves to everyone, we have little self-respect.

Ultimately, God breaks down the artificial walls by which we justify ourselves. That sorry task of self-justification cannot be compared to the art of constructing those walls that provide us a modicum of safety. For example, many people are patriotic and favor their own country over others. God's sanctuary, however, transcends the particularity of any flag or other symbols that we fashion as walls.

The walls that God breaks down are those by which we validate our own worth, and are largely symbolic. More than anything else, walls that we create are nothing other than idols. An idol is an ardent, excessive impostor. And God smashes idols.

No more walls! At the most fundamental level, in Jesus Christ, my neighbor and I share in the peace and love of God. This is the unity that breaks down the dividing hostility that separates us. God promises to provide. What my neighbor is given does not detract from my need or security. In that promise, I can be at peace with my neighbor, and my neighbor with me.

What is beyond the walls that God shatters? Indeed, to what degree can I find myself in another and another in myself?

Aristotle instructed us that a friend is a "second self."

Even my enemy indicates my shadow-self that I cannot accept. Therefore, even my enemy shows my need for a Savior and that I can rest in God's life-giving peace between us.

Reach out, O Great Redeemer, and save us from the fear and self-ishness that divide us. Break down the barriers that inhibit good will amongst the peoples of the world. Heal those hearts damaged by both new and age-old animosities. It is in accepting and loving one another that we come to know you. It is in knowing you that we are all made one. So be it.

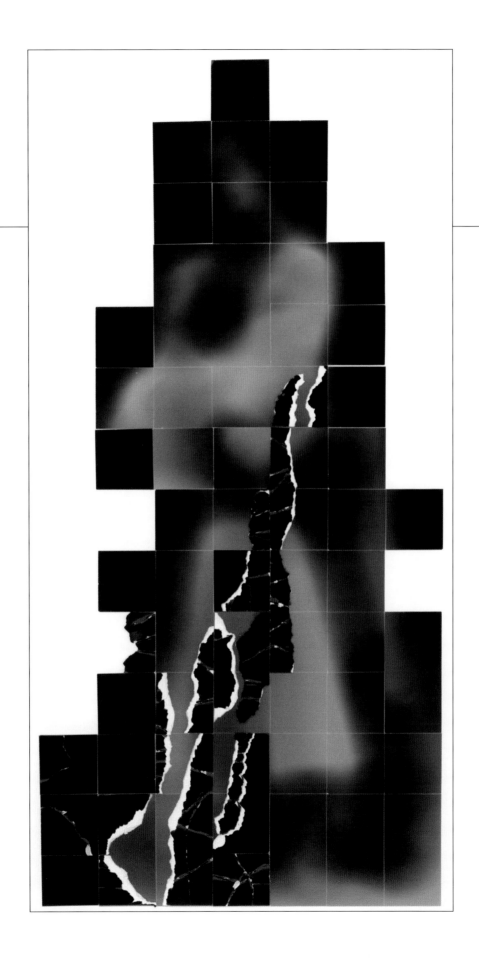

Social Health

Our culture tends to confuse peace with tolerance. We almost instinctively assume that we are peaceful if we are tolerant, and belligerent if we are intolerant. The question of tolerance, however, masks a problem. Tolerance all too often is disguised indifference. Tolerance suggests that, provided I do no harm to another, whatever I do is okay. I can even choose to harm myself, if I see fit.

Tolerance does not demand that a nation shapes its weapons into plowshares. Rather, it allows one to point a loaded weapon at others, just so long as a shot isn't fired. Tolerance is détente, a disguising of tension between nations or any other group of people. It is, perhaps, better than outright conflict, but it falls short of the peace that God aims for the world.

Roman Catholic philosopher John Courtney Murray said that disagreement is a difficult thing to reach. His point was that disagreement is a hard fought goal that is preferable to violence.

Of course, people can agree to disagree, but to do so brings the conversation to a close. To do so may ignore strengths that fail to be exercised if we choose to end the discussion. Even those traditions, such as the church's theology or the liberal arts, that support us, as philosopher Alasdair MacIntyre said, are themselves arguments over the nature of the tradition.

Traditions that we embody and hold dear are always negotiating their life as they press into our callings in the contemporary world. We share in that negotiation, especially as we aim to be faithful to such traditions. The traditions that sustain us are fragile. Yet they give us strength as we deal with the ambiguity that daily surrounds us.

Life itself is often uncertain. For no other reason, all people, at some level or another, walk by faith. Nonetheless, we are always tempted to believe sight is a preferable way by which to walk.

In the end, only faith can accept life's fragility because it commits life into the care of a merciful God. When we exchange the peace in church, "the peace of the Lord be with you," faith shares this truth physically and socially. It acknowledges the power of God's peace to sustain community. Such power is not over others, but is shared between one another.

In the exchange of peace, we move beyond tolerance to agreement. Our agreement is that in this fragile, fractured, and uncertain world, we are ambassadors, sent on a mission with God's peace, given person-to-person, in God's social health.

Rescue our spirits, Faithful Lord, from the temptations and uncertainties of life and make us whole. Save us, especially, from insensitivity and resignation to the cries of our brothers and sisters in need. Help us to become people of vision and instruments of change. Strengthen our faith in you so that your love may shine more brightly in our hearts and in our actions. Amen.

Ministry to the Poor

Jesus noted, "the poor you have with you always" (John 12:8).

St. Paul confessed, "I have learned to be content with all things" (Philippians 4:11).

At one time, Christians thought, as long as someone's soul is saved, what difference does it make whether or not one is poor?

The fact that the poor will always be with us should not be used as an excuse to justify poverty. Some people are poor because of apathy, indolence, or inactivity. Others are poor because of mental illness or chemical dependency. Others are poor because the economy and other societal structures are not designed to favor those who start life's race from behind.

We cannot pit body and soul against each other. God is the creator of both and loves both.

The church has a ministry to the poor. It has a ministry to all. We cannot ignore the poor by focusing solely on changing the social dynamics of poverty and be satisfied.

So, how can we who are wealthy build solidarity with the poor? First, we must understand that regardless of how much wealth we have, our own souls can be poor. We might have the poverty of judgmentalism or indifference to others. In that sense, anyone is only a step away from poverty, no matter how financially secure they might be. Second, unlike some medieval views, we must recognize that poverty is not holy. It brings no higher status with God. Third, we must understand that where it is found, poverty is an invitation to us for service and growth. It is an opportunity to learn from those who deal with deepest poverty and to help improve their life situation. Finally, as little Christs to our neighbors we must seek to improve those social structures that unfairly favor some over others.

The man in a parka is one image of the poor, neglected, or marginalized. Here the parka hides the man's eyes. However, his smile is a window into his soul. One can have all things taken away and yet not be among the worst of the poor. To paraphrase Victor Frankl, one can have everything taken from one, yet one can still decide on how one will carry dignity and find meaning in one's circumstances. No poverty can take this decision away from us as long as we have full use of our mental faculties.

Contentment with life's wealth provides a foundation that permits us to make the most of our lives. God intends that we develop our potential for God's glory and for the well-being of our neighbor.

When we understand that we are not the star around which the universe circles, we can find our place within the universe's cycles and histories. In that, we become free. In freedom, we are never poor. When we receive our daily bread, we receive enough.

Lord God, we live in a world marked by the generosity of your creation as well as a world that grows increasingly more divided by those who have and those who do not. Bless those who are poor in spirit and in the necessities of life and those who cannot care for themselves or who have been marginalized by our actions and our abundance. Turn our hearts and our energies to acts of service to them. Help us to remember that we need not have less in order for others to have more. Amen.

Homeless

We've all heard the phrase, "there, but for the grace of God, go I." That sentiment, however, rarely testifies to the grace of God. It can twist a confession of God's grace into an expression of one's own self-righteousness, or luck.

To be confronted by the homeless is often uncomfortable for us. In this image, the face of the homeless man is hidden from us. It is the very symbol of the facelessness that poverty can and does indeed create. The homeless can teach us that we are never wholly secure—that anyone is within a day of the fate of being homeless. With that fear staring us in the face, how likely are we to turn from the homeless?

Jesus tells us, "Blessed are you who are poor, for yours is the kingdom of God" (Luke 6:20). Jesus acknowledges that the poor are not to be blamed. The poor cannot be held accountable for accessing wealth or a power that they do not have. Nevertheless, to be without a home is to be without security and eventually an identity.

We are pilgrims and strangers on earth. We all need a home with its network of support (emotional, economic, social, religious, and psychological), if we are to survive and live. The homeless lack these basic human needs.

Those of us who read this volume are among the wealthiest on earth. We know the security of three meals a day. Often, our response to the homeless can run the gamut from revulsion to engagement and service. More deeply, our response to the homeless indicates where we stand with respect to our own poverty, our own emptiness. We despise our own uncomfortable emptiness because of the anxiety it evokes within us. We flee to our power, charisma, wit, and status to bolster a sagging self-worth.

Whether we like it or not, God reduces all to some type of "nothingness." This is not because God is spiteful. Rather, it is because God will have us trust in nothing but God's own goodness. When all the props of false self-security are taken from us, only then can we find our homecoming in God. No other assurance is more certain than that which does not avoid death, but rather comes through it, and is up-righted on the other side. That is a life lived from a theology of the cross. The resurrection victory of Jesus through the cross is our victory because our being in him is through faith.

How do I see the homeless, now that my emptiness and poverty are tamed in Jesus' death and resurrection? Are the homeless, in one way or another, my sister and brother?

Forgive us, Faithful God, for our insensitivity to the homeless and those who lack the necessities of life that so many of us take for granted and enjoy in abundance. Save us, especially, from those attitudes and judgments that prevent us from seeing and serving those who are homeless—the poor in spirit as well as those who lack adequate shelter and food. Help us, also, to confront the homelessness that exists in our own lives. May our hope for the future rest in your eternal promise to be with us always. Amen.

Enough

There is an adage that says you are what you eat. We cringe. Surely we are more than something physical.

In Mexico, corn embodies the people; and the people of Mexico, for the most part, celebrate corn. From Mexican farmers we can discern the following truth. If there is no corn, there are no people. If there is no corn, you do not eat. If you do not eat, you will not be. Apart from the energy that drives life, we starve. In starvation, dreams die and despair is born.

In America, corn, too, is fundamental to our way of life. Corn sustains us—and even some of our humor.

There are 800 million people in the world who need food. They cry out the question of immense importance…*is there enough to go around?*

The earth does not have infinite resources, but God does. We must not pit the limitations of the earth against the needs of the starving. To the question: *is there enough to go around?* The answer is, yes, there is enough. The heart of the matter is: why do we refuse to share? No human being deserves to starve.

Jesus tells us, "Give and it shall be given to you; good measure, pressed down, shaken together, overflowing" (Luke 6:38). That calls us to do the right thing. No reward is needed for doing that. If we were not self-centered, we would naturally be generous. We lose nothing when we give, because we have already received abundantly. We don't share when we fear that we won't have enough. This fear, though, isn't the truth. The truth is that God will provide.

Every community on earth has an image or face. Corn is something both Mexicans and Americans share. Indeed, we are what we eat, not because materialism is true, but because as N. F. S. Grundtvig put it, *the entire earth*, and not just the human, *bears the image of God.* That truth should humble us a little.

God provides. We hoard. In our twisted imagination, wants become needs, and needs become entitlements.

The barriers we erect to make our wealth legitimate are arbitrary. In God's fields there are no fences. God's property lacks a "no trespassing" sign. God knows no artificial boundaries established by our quests for domination. In sharing, we are free from fear and self-centeredness. Our earthly gifts must serve all the people of God's good creation. Always!

Generous God, we rejoice and give thanks for the goodness and abundance of your creation. Help us to become faithful stewards of that bounty—both in caring for and in sharing what you have made. Let your weekly invitation to the Lord's Table: "All is ready; come to the feast that has been prepared for you" become our daily admonition to share what we have with others. Let it be so.

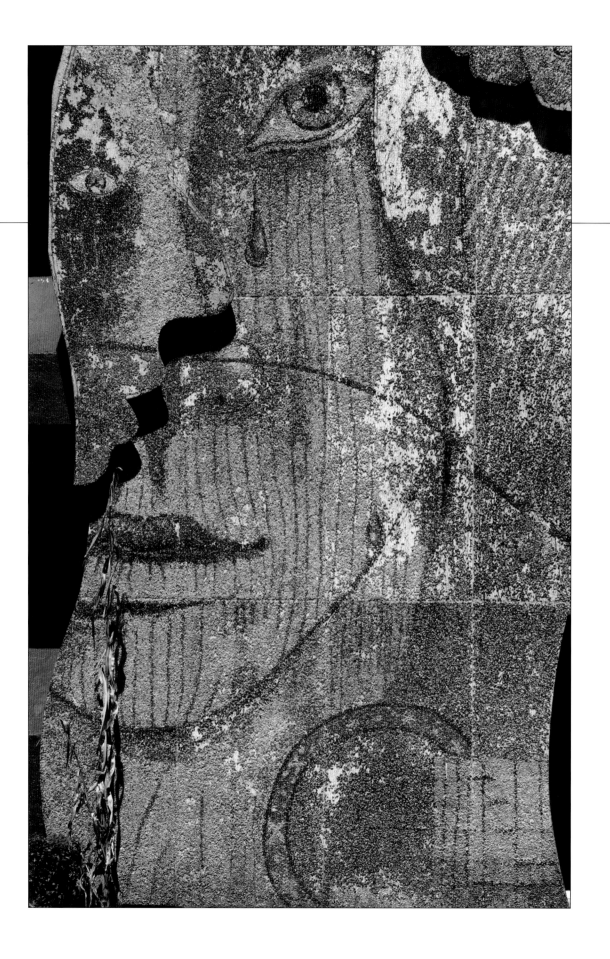

Question

To the Jewish people and throughout history, the event will always be remembered as Kristalnacht, the "night of broken glass." It was the night in which the Nazis began destroying the Jewish-owned businesses and local synagogues, and which progressed to a yet more evil end. It was also a night in which the lives of individuals, families, and communities were shattered. Symbolically, the night of broken glass reminds us, in light of our image, that "glass" shatters in more than one way. Glass and lives became shattered in violence ignited by a current of anxiety made manifest as hate.

The energy of one people was directed hatefully to destroy another. Ultimately, energy unleashed as hate destroyed the lives of six million Jews, and millions of others as well. It also provoked a counter-energy that brought opposition from other nations that would eventually defeat the Nazis.

The Holocaust was a result of anger. Such anger, however, is simply cloaked anxiety. Anger is socially acceptable. We justify it by a righteous cause. Anxiety, though, is seldom acceptable. Fear evokes fear in others. Who wants to deal with another's fear?

Often we justify behaviors that result from anger, but faith must always seek to "discern the spirits" (1 John 4:1)—an important task of the church. We are not to believe every spirit, but instead to *test* the spirits to see whether they come from God.

"The window is broken and it cannot be closed." Those who remember the cold war between the United States and the Soviet Union know of another situation when broken glass was involved. In this case, though, it became a symbol of liberation.

Power in the Soviet Union had been moved so far away from the repressive government and into the people's hands that the Russian Archpriest Victor Petluchenko noted, "The window is broken and it cannot be closed." Quietly, resourcefully, and intentionally, the source of that transformation was an unlikely lot, the babushkas, the intellectuals, and the artists. These three contributed the most energy to the downfall of the Soviet leadership.

When is a social movement an expression of violence and when is it an act of liberation? By what standard do we measure the success that leads to creative social transformation? In the midst of social upheaval, how can we be sure? Perhaps the only thing of which we can be sure is that we must unremittingly question. Otherwise, we will never be able to discern the truth we need.

The power of any person, people, or nation that governs must admit that only so much control can be maintained. In dealing with people, we are forced to admit that our control is always limited. That is another reason why faith is so crucial for a healthful life. God's creative, transforming Spirit blows where he will. Once we discern a movement as creative we need to find our place in it for the common good.

It is a shame that windows had to break. It would be better if we would allow the creative Spirit to move us simply to open the window.

Eternal God, liberate us from the suspicion and ignorance that separates us from you and from one another. Help us to reject those thoughts and behaviors that result from disappointment and anger and oftentimes promote fear and anxiety in others. As heirs of the reformation spirit, let us speak out boldly against injustice and discrimination. Open the windows of our lives so that your creative and transforming Spirit might blow through. Amen.

Tohu Wabohu

With the Word all things began,
Life in ocean, life on land;
With the word were man and woman
Raised from dust, created human,
Prince of earth and child of God.

When the soul of man was stirred
By a breath divine, the Word
Was in heart of man created;
This on earth inaugurated
Human life and history.

Not the clever hand or brain
Can humanity explain.
For its secret is the spirit;
Only in the Word we hear it,
Self-revealing, heaven-born.

Only in the Word ascends
Man beyond the life that ends;
In the Word he breaks his prisons,
Soars aloft to higher visions,
Comprehends eternity.*

God's word not only describes and directs, but also creates. In God's word, order—a space and time for life and community to flourish—is spoken.

Our world is orderly and structured. Everyday, people go to work, to school, eat, dress, and participate in games and amusements. Life can seem to have a rhythm, even if things become hectic or chaotic.

Despite such order, there are apocalyptic themes found in popular culture. We find ourselves entertained by stories that describe the end of our planet, whether that be by asteroids hitting it, aliens invading it, atomic or biological annihilation, or ecological disaster.

We fear chaos! Who doesn't? If the world were coming to an end, how could one raise a family, obtain the necessities for living, or progress in the pursuit of happiness?

Some Christians thrive from a sense of the world's ending. They have the stages of Christ's return charted and mapped ahead of time (as if the Bible were offering us a map!). Thereby they presume that they can judge winners and losers from God's perspective.

The threat of chaos seems to be a shadow from which we cannot separate ourselves. But, remember that it was from the chaos, from the formlessness and void, the *tohu wabohu*, as the Hebrew in Genesis 1:2 puts it, that God creates the world.

That formlessness and void was threatening, but it was the potential from which God created all things, and that creation was very good. It was from that apparent mayhem that God called forth, from nothing (*ex nihilo*), the mystery that is the galaxies, the universe, and the conditions for life itself.

Must we fear chaos? With God going before us, leading the way, we know that "all things work together for good to those who love God" (Romans 8:28). Chaos we need not fear. God ever invites us to life-enhancing, life-sustaining possibilities even in the darkest chaotic moments.

Even in those personal times of chaos and seeming nothingness, God continues to craft us into people of faith, called to works of love. Creation, not chaos, is always both God's first and last word.

*(Søren Damsgaard Rodholm, adapting N. F. S. Grundtvig's poetry)

Author of Life, in the beginning, before the dawn of time, you created the heavens and the earth and all creatures that dwell therein. Out of chaos, you brought order to the planets and life to our being. Yet, sometimes, we struggle with making sense out of your plan for us and for creation. Let us not be disappointed or frightened by that struggle for we know that you are within and beside us and continue to shape our identity in your image. Thanks be to God. Amen.

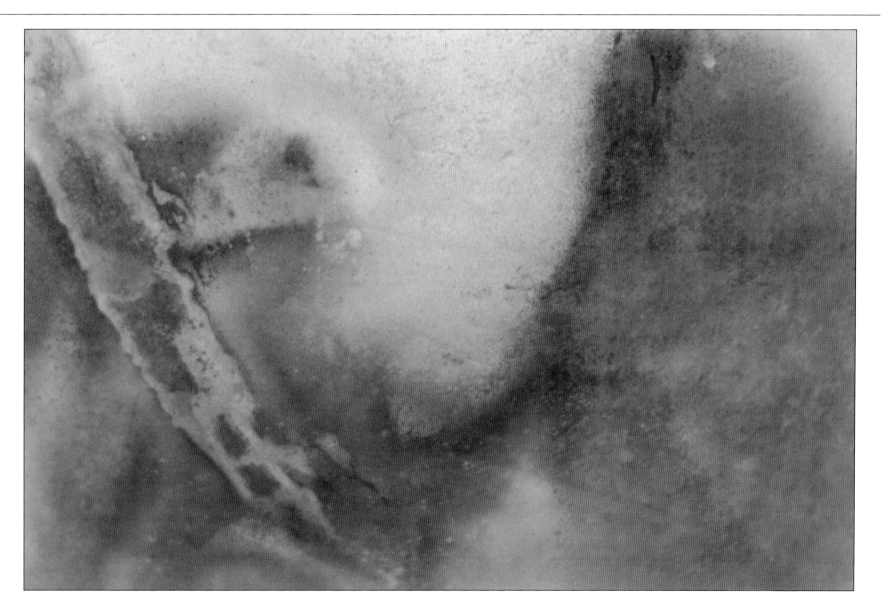

Uniqueness

"Do your own thing" has been the mantra of the last fifty years. While it's not said as frequently as it was in the sixties, it continues to haunt our culture in one way or another. In the nine-teenth-century, Alexis de Tocqueville had already identified the American push for individualism. Self-fulfillment is found in defin-ing oneself for oneself. Ironically, in this very quest to establish their own unique, individual personalities, Americans tend to mimic their peers. Young people, for example, wear the same brands of clothing, seek similar body piercings, or tattoos. The more we seek to be our own persons, the more we copy others. The more we seek to establish our own individuality, the more we are entrapped in the expectations of the herd.

In contrast to this American herd instinct, to seek to estab-lish one's own unique gifts and talents is a God-given calling. In the church, we are many members yet one body. If the body is to function well, not all members should do the same thing. But, they are all interdependent on each other. They receive their abili-ty to establish their own unique gifts and talents because they are upheld by others.

We often feel alone—even the more so when we try to con-form to expectations of others. But, in the new life in Christ, we are never truly alone. We are always upheld by the Spirit in the Body of Christ, the church. That truth is not always at the forefront of our thinking, imagining, or doing. Yet it is no less true. The church, across the ages and throughout the world, bears witness to Christ's Spirit which is our lifeline to God.

The more we seek to fulfill ourselves as our sole venture, the more we find ourselves defeated. Total self-centeredness under-mines life itself. Instead, seeking the common good, we find our unique gifts and identity in rapport with others. It is this dynamic between our attachment with others and our detachment from oth-ers which allows God's beauty to shine through us.

God of Mystery, we pray, this day and everyday, that you will continue your creative work within and through us. You have crafted each and every one of us in your own image and gifted us with many and varied talents. Help us to recognize and honor the unique-ness of these talents. Guide, also, our use of these gifts that we may, together, employ them wisely in greater service to you and to one another. Amen.

Evening Sun

Teach me, gentle flowers,
To wait for springtime showers,
In this winter world to grow,
Green and strong beneath the snow!
Teach me, gentle flowers!

Teach me lonely heather,
Where songbirds nest together,
Though my life should seem unblest,
To keep a song within my breast!
Teach me, lonely heather!

Mighty ocean, teach me,
To do the task that needs me,
And reflect, as days depart,
Heaven's peace within my heart!
Mighty ocean, teach me!

Shady lanes, refreshing,
Teach me to be a blessing
To some weary soul each day,
Friends or foes who pass my way!
Shady lanes, refreshing!

Evening sun, descending,
Teach me, when life is ending,
Night shall pass and I, like you,
Shall rise again, where life is new!
Teach me, sun descending!*

*(Danish Hymn by Christian Richardt, translated by Søren Damsgaard Rodholm)

Teach me, Radiant Lord, to put my trust in your abiding love. Teach me to savor the beauty and promise of each moment with the assurance that more is yet to come. Teach me to understand and embrace the tasks you set before me to do. Teach me to walk in the newness of life that your death on the cross makes possible. Teach me, Lord, to await the evening sun. Teach me, Lord. Amen.

Glory

Finish then thy new creation,
Pure and spotless let us be;
Let us see thy great salvation
Perfectly restored in thee!
Changed from glory into glory,
Till in heaven we take our place,
Till we cast our crowns before thee,
Lost in wonder, love, and praise!*

Charles Wesley's words, describing our journey to paradise, aptly spark our imagination: what will eternal life be like?

We cannot help but pose this question and yet we know that its answer is entirely beyond our comprehension.

We can only accept the invitation of the victorious Christ in the Book of Revelation: "the Spirit and the Bride say, 'come'." We are invited to a celestial city, a diverse community of angels, archangels, cherubim, seraphim, and all the company of heaven, all embraced in the triune God. Encircling God, surrounded by the twenty-four elders, who are the twelve apostles and the twelve tribes of Israel (Revelation 4), our joy will be fulfilled; our Sabbath rest will give total refreshment.

The continuum between that life and this is nothing less than a continuing journey into mystery.

Free from sin, how much more beauty will we discover? What further color and texture will there be to enjoy?

The circle, around which the church triumphant flows, is not vicious but virtuous. It opens horizons to newness and adventure. We will see the reign of Christ as a royal priesthood.

Christians love God for God's own sake. At the same time, we are also grateful for all God's gifts, the promise of eternal life, the forgiveness of sins, community, and outreach.

All these support us on this journey until that calling in which we are lost in wonder, love, and praise.

*(Charles Wesley, *Lutheran Book of Worship*, # 315)

King of Glory, in baptism you claimed us as your own and welcomed us into your family and into life's journey. Through the word and the sacraments and the company of one another you continued to guide our earthly journey. And, finally at life's end, we know that you stand ready to receive us into eternal life. We give thanks, always, for your unfailing love and for your sacrifice on the cross which secured for us the gift of eternal life. "Jesus Christ is the first born of the Lord; to him be glory and power forever and ever. Amen. Alleluia."

Concluding Thought

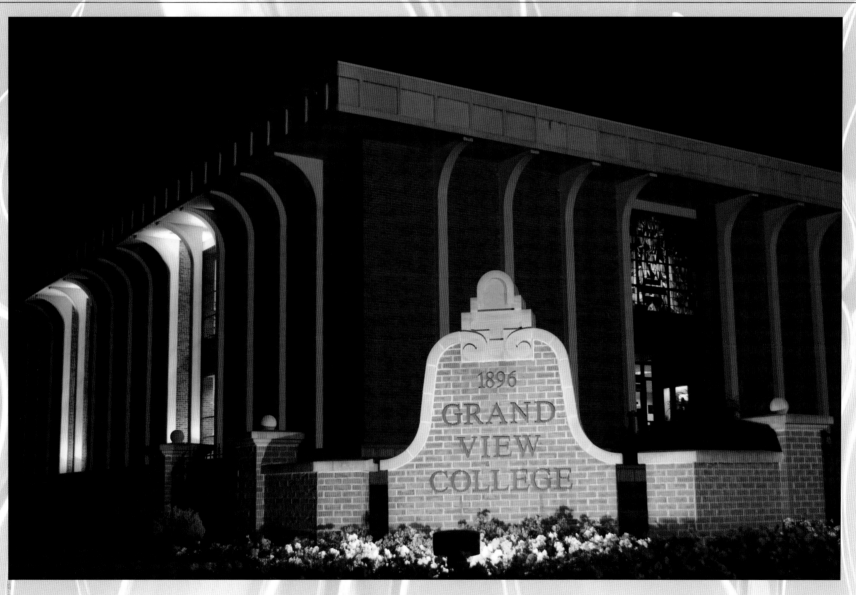

1896
GRAND
VIEW
COLLEGE

A Gift of Vocation

In this volume, we encounter two overarching truths. First, we receive our identity from God's communication to us in the world. This identity, which is granted in freedom, de-centers us from the urge for consumption and control. Second, Jesus' cross, whose power we receive in baptism, ends the quest for self-security. It was our quest for self-security that put Jesus to death in the first place. We could not tolerate his embrace of sinners. It threatened our status quo. God, however, has the final say. In Jesus' resurrection we are renewed, opened to God, ourselves, neighbors, and the earth.

Those two truths, at the heart of Christian faith and articulated deeply by Lutheran theology, bring unity to the photographic images and written reflections in this book.

The authors of this book are two ordained pastors and two dedicated laymen. Corporately they bring their gifts as teachers, theologians, pastors, photographer, students, artist, administrators, and writers to their chosen task of reflecting on our identity, God's communication with us, and the cross of Jesus.

Reflections are not meant for quick perusal. Reflections may be read or viewed repeatedly. They are meant to be pondered, to be savored, to be integrated into our lives over a period of time. These reflections may be viewed, read, and reread, with the expectation that insights may become apparent and truths may be revealed.

The seven themes of the book pull us in and hold onto us as we discover more and more each time we open the book. Spirituality of Communication, Newness of the New Life, Fragmentation and Wholeness, Ministry as Service, Renewal in the Midst of Conflict, Vocation, and Alpha and Omega are the guideposts to our discernment. They can be taken as a whole or pulled out according to our need on any particular day. The more we discover and learn, the more we realize that we have only begun to uncover a small portion of the spiritual resources available to us.

I am grateful for the heritage of Grand View College. As a college of the church, Grand View has given a particular gift of vocational vitality to those who have been blessed by being touched by its ethos. The impact of Nicolai F. S. Grundtvig and the Danish Lutheran appreciation for vocation in daily living and for God's presence in creation are richly reflected in this volume. Today, Grand View is renewing a partnership with the church which will enrich both college and church in faithfulness as well as learning.

The writers and photographer who have produced this volume represent the creative result of the meeting of faith, learning, art, and vocation in the receiving of and proclamation of God's Word for us.

Bishop Philip L. Hougen

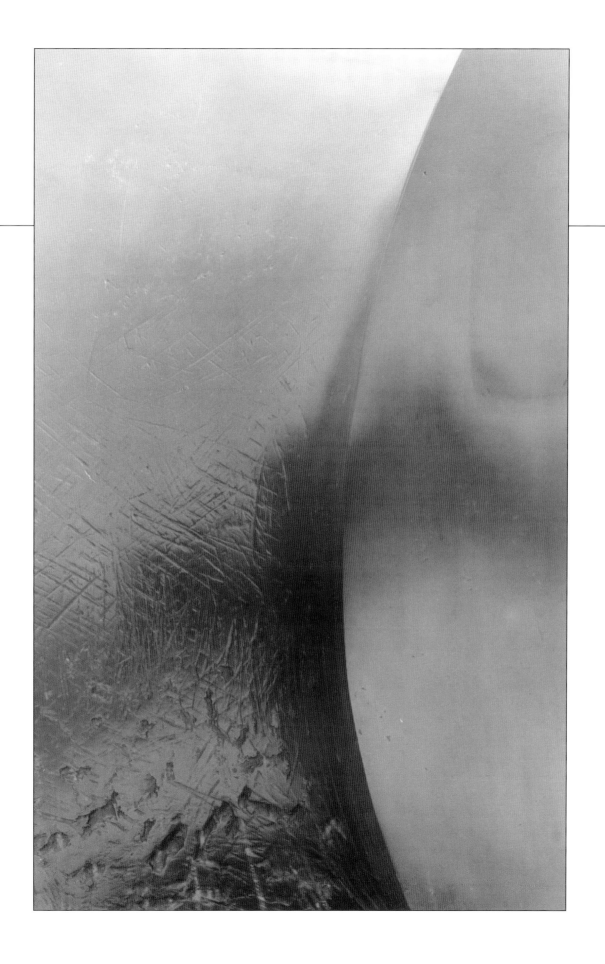

Acknowledgments

In the venture of producing this book of images, meditations, and prayers, there are many from whom the authors received much encouragement and help. The following persons especially have assisted the authors. They have our gratitude.

First, we are grateful to the Division for Global Mission and the Division for Ministry of the Evangelical Lutheran Church in America for sponsoring us at the Global Mission Event in Milwaukee, Wisconsin during the summer of 2004. At that event, the primary authors, as a teaching theologian and as a parish pastor and photographer, were invited to conduct a workshop on the theme: Imaging Luther's Theology of the Cross. That presentation gave impetus to the collaborative vision from which these meditations grew.

We thank President Kent L. Henning of Grand View College for introducing this volume with an insightful Foreword. We share his vision that honors artistic, academic, and spiritual endeavors in both higher education and in the church at large. Likewise, we thank Provost Ronald L. Taylor for crafting the prayers that enhance and graciously convey the spirit of each meditation. Appreciation also goes to Philip L. Hougen, Bishop, Southeastern Iowa Synod, for his interest and commitment in the life and history of Grand View College and its continuing mission in higher education. His concluding thought radiates the partnership between the church, learning, and heritage that calls us to discern new horizons for daily life and ministry.

We have found Grand View College to provide a stimulating environment for reflection on the interchange between ministry and teaching. Grand View College encourages its community to grapple simultaneously with the life of the world, the life of the mind, and the life of faith. While engagement with many students, faculty, staff, friends, and alumni have advanced our work, we especially honor Kathryn Pohlmann Duffy, Professor of Music, and Kenneth Sundet Jones, Associate Professor of Religion, for their meticulous reading and helpful suggestions that have improved the manuscript. Additionally, Carol Hall's secretarial expertise helped the manuscript progress smoothly. And we are grateful to Paul Rorem, Professor of Church History at Princeton Seminary, who offered a final read that gives this work a quality that we can only treasure.

Jack and Betty Smith of Muscatine, Iowa repeatedly copyedited the manuscript in its early stages, offering numerous insights that have made it more pleasing and inviting. Likewise, Deborah Darge sharpened our language and concepts with her skilled poetic sensitivities. Shirley Bessinger, Diana Darge, Rebecca Christensen, and Cynthia Cort unceasingly encouraged both the pursuit of the arts and the pursuits of teaching and pastoral ministry. Betty Joan Nyquist Mattes and Lydia Anna Volz, each in their own ways, provided assistance that helped move this project forward. In addition, Carol Marie Mattes, together with Joseph, Peter, and Emma, generously gave time, energy, and enthusiasm to see this project completed from start to finish.

The following individuals and organizations have graciously contributed towards the costs of publication: Shirley Bessinger, Diana Darge, Deborah G. Darge, Abigail and Ben, John Anthony and Cynthia Cort, Dennis and Rebecca Christensen, Harold and Lara Kramme, Ken and Alice Rasmussen, Duane and Vinette Skow, Delores Jespersen, Louis and Elaine Bredesky, Virgil and Janice Jacobsen, Central Iowa Associates of the American-Scandinavian Foundation (Barbara Lund, president), Rhodes Consultation on the Future of Church Related Higher Education, Thrivent Financial for Lutherans, the Southeastern Iowa Synod, Luther Memorial Church (Des Moines, Iowa), Grace Lutheran Church Endowment Fund (Des Moines, Iowa), Danish Brotherhood Lodge 15 (Marlin Nielsen, president), and Grand View College.

The cover design by Jesse Hubbard uses the Grand View College President's Medallion created by Ann Au.

The making of this manuscript is the result of conversations with those above, but the authors are indebted also to many who are not named here. Let it be noted that silently they continue to speak.

Leonard Flachman, Lutheran University Press, thorough and kind leadership has helped guide the author's throughout the publication process.

Finally, the authors sincerely desire that each participant be honored in the partnered strength, cooperative compassion, and mutual encouragement that have guided us throughout. To God alone the glory.

About the Authors

Ronald R. Darge
is an ordained pastor of the Evangelical Lutheran Church in America and a professional photographer. He holds masters degrees from Drake University and from Central Lutheran Theological Seminary (now the Lutheran School of Theology in Chicago) and has served parishes in Michigan and Iowa, and as an Adjunct Instructor of Photography and Religion at Grand View College in Des Moines, Iowa.

Mark C. Mattes
currently chairs the Departments of Philosophy and Religion at Grand View College. Prior to this, as an ordained ELCA pastor, he served parishes in Illinois and Wisconsin. He holds the doctorate from the University of Chicago and is the author of *The Role of Justification in Contemporary Theology* and has co-edited *A More Radical Gospel* and *The Preached God*.

Ronald L. Taylor
serves as the Provost and Vice President for Academic Affairs at Grand View College. He holds the doctorate from Case Western Reserve University. He has served as Dean of Continuing Studies and later as Executive Assistant to the President at Ursuline College in Cleveland, Ohio. Prior to coming to Grand View, he was Dean of the College at Lake Erie College in Painesville, Ohio.

Kent L. Henning
serves as the President of Grand View College. He holds a master's degree from Duke University and previously served in the Advancement Office of Carthage College in Kenosha, Wisconsin, Duke University, George Mason University in Fairfax, Virginia, and Wartburg College in Waverly, Iowa.

Philip L. Hougen
serves as the Bishop of the Southeastern Iowa Synod of the ELCA. He holds a doctorate of ministry degree from the Lutheran School of Theology in Chicago and previously served several congregations in Iowa and Illinois, most recently as the Senior Pastor of Grace Lutheran Church in Des Moines, Iowa.